RHS

How Can I
HELP
HEDGEHOGS?

RHS How Can I Help Hedgehogs?
Authors: Helen Bostock and Sophie Collins
First published in Great Britain in 2019 by Mitchell Beazley, an imprint of
Octopus Publishing Group Ltd, Carmelite House, 50 Victoria Embankment,
London EC4Y 0DZ
www.octopusbooks.co.uk

An Hachette UK Company
www.hachette.co.uk

Published in association with the Royal Horticultural Society
Copyright © Quarto Publishing plc 2019

ISBN: 978 1 78472 6218

A CIP record of this book is available from the British Library
Set in Archer and Open Sans
Printed and bound in China

Conceived, designed and produced by
The Bright Press
Part of the Quarto Group
Ovest House
58 West Street
Brighton
BN1 2RA
England
Publisher: Mark Searle
Creative Director: James Evans
Managing Editor: Jacqui Sayers
Editor: Emily Angus
Design: Lindsey Johns
Mitchell Beazley Publisher: Alison Starling
RHS Head of Editorial: Chris Young
RHS Publisher: Rae Spencer-Jones
RHS Consultant Editor: Simon Maughan
RHS Consultant Editor: Guy Barter

The Royal Horticultural Society is the UK's leading gardening charity
dedicated to advancing horticulture and promoting good gardening.
Its charitable work includes providing expert advice and information,
training the next generation of gardeners, creating hands-on opportunities
for children to grow plants and conducting research into plants, pests
and environmental issues affecting gardeners.

For more information visit www.rhs.org.uk or call 0845 130 4646.

RHS

How Can I
HELP
HEDGEHOGS?

A Gardener's Collection
of Inspiring Ideas *for*
Welcoming Wildlife

HELEN BOSTOCK & SOPHIE COLLINS

FOREWORD BY ISABELLA TREE

MITCHELL
BEAZLEY

Contents

1 In the Air

2 On (and in) the Ground

3 Water in the Garden

4 Hands-on Help

5 The Bigger Picture

Foreword

BY ISABELLA TREE

Private gardens in Britain cover over 10 million acres – an area larger than all the country's nature reserves combined. The potential of these millions of gardens, large and small, to provide habitat for wildlife is immense. Every garden owner can make a difference, and this wonderful book shows us how.

Never has there been a greater need to support British wildlife. Over the last few years, reports on the state of nature in Britain have been unremittingly dire. According to the RSPB, we have 40 million fewer birds

The best bug hotels have lots of small spaces in different shapes and sizes and are generally made from different reclaimed materials, or natural objects found in the garden.

in our skies today than we did in the 1960s. Native wild flowers are being lost at a rate of nearly one species a year per county – and that loss is accelerating. Insect numbers have halved since 1970. Gone are the days of midge and moth splatterings on car windscreens. Moths have declined by 88 per cent, ground beetles 72 per cent and butterflies 76 per cent. Bees and other pollinators are in crisis. And these are just the species that can be identified and monitored. Countless other insects, water plants, lichens, mosses and fungi are not even on the radar.

It's tempting to be distracted by ecological headlines elsewhere – the chain-sawing of tropical rainforests, the construction of hydro-electric dams, the pollution of our seas – but what has been happening in the British Isles over the past three decades has been just as damaging. According to the 2016 State of Nature report, the UK is one of the most nature-depleted countries in the world, ranked 29th lowest out of 218 countries. What brings this home more poignantly than anything is the disappearance, in recent years, of some of our once common and most-loved species like house sparrows, water voles, dormice and hedgehogs.

Yet all is not lost. Rising to meet these unwelcome revelations is a groundswell of concern and a genuine desire to do something positive. From Extinction Rebellion to the anti-plastic revolution, we are beginning to think more deeply about our impact on the planet, to look differently at the landscape around us and find ways in which we can reverse the declines.

Most of us have influence over vegetation of some description, be it garden, allotment, roadside verge or window box. Simply mowing the lawn less frequently and reducing pesticide and fertiliser use can yield exponential benefits for wildlife. But how much more rewarding – and entertaining – to actively encourage bees and butterflies, birds and small mammals into our own back yard through establishing habitat, selecting plants and providing nesting places. *How Can I Help Hedgehogs?* shows us how we can do this, by providing fascinating insights into the life-cycles and habits of our native bugs and birds and revealing a whole universe at our fingertips, waiting to spring to life.

Gardens, this book reveals, are where human beings – just like ants and earthworms and beavers – can be a keystone species, adapting, nurturing, tweaking the habitat to the optimum for life. We can play with the mix: welcoming in wild flowers amongst our exotics and into our lawns; providing winter and spring sources of nectar for early pollinators; using natural processes like nematodes and companion-planting to counteract 'pests' like aphids and greenfly; leaving the odd pile of leaves for hibernating hedgehogs; or a patch of nettles for butterflies. This is rewilding at micro-level, and much is about changing our aesthetic: learning to relax a little about tidiness; perhaps even allowing ourselves to be consciously messy in areas where we feel it doesn't matter too much.

And if we can connect with our neighbours the rewards can multiply further. If every garden in a street cuts a hedgehog hole in the fence, suddenly a street becomes a wildlife corridor. And a row of back-gardens can connect with a park, or a railway embankment, or a tow-path along a river, and out into the wider countryside, plugging in to the life-support system for our wildlife countrywide.

This book is a box of delights, a toolkit to enhance our enjoyment of nature on our doorstep and provide countless hours of fascination and rapture in the place where we most like to potter and tinker and, ultimately, be at one with the world.

■ Introduction

HUMAN SOCIETY IS WAKING UP to the need to safeguard other species. Where better to do this than in our own backyards? In recent decades, numbers of hedgehogs, wild bees and other common or garden species have plummeted alarmingly so there's not a day to lose to transform our gardens into nature reserves. Thankfully, being stewards of nature has never been so easy or well-informed. *How Can I Help Hedgehogs?* is a friendly, uplifting look at some of the challenges, conundrums and curiosities of wildlife gardening.

It's Elemental

Gardens are spaces we use for growing vegetables, drying the washing, enjoying barbecues, letting the kids play and more. But how does wildlife see gardens? To them they are just another type of habitat. Or, to be more accurate, a whole host of habitats, since each of us garden slightly differently. To help get into this mindset, we start by breaking the garden down into its key elements: air, land and water.

Creatures at home in the air include bats (the only mammals that can fly), our feathered friends and hundreds of species of flying insects and invertebrates. Did you realize your security lighting can be impacting on nocturnal inhabitants? And that feeding birds year round is more

▼ Choosing plants that will appeal to as many different kinds of insect as possible is key to increasing the wildlife diversity in your garden.

QUICK ANSWERS

The 'A' box under each question offers you the quick and dirty answer in the shortest form possible. Read on for the main text, which offers additional context and plenty of extra detail.

barley straw and a rainwater butt can keep your pond in tip top condition for wildlife. But it's not all about ponds. If you live in an area prone to flash floods, then a Rain Garden could be just the ticket.

Garden Wildlife Rescue Party

By now, we are well on our way to becoming champion wildlife gardeners. So it's time to get properly hands on with the help. But doing the right thing by wildlife isn't always as straight forward as it might seem. Who hasn't ever felt a bit conflicted over how to deal with garden 'pests'? Or wondered what to do with an injured wild animal? Build your confidence in finding pesticide-free ways of gardening, handling difficult situations and coming to the rescue of wildlife in distress.

helpful than sporadic feeding? Chances are you've already picked up that single flowers are better for bees than doubles, but have you ever stopped to wonder why? This first chapter answers some of those niggling questions.

Next we explore the needs of the land lovers. Learn how to make a hedgehog door, build a beetle bank and turn your compost into a cosy reptile nursery. Tiger worms, woodlice and tiny springtails are also residents of the compost heap, but did you realize we would be buried under feet of rotting leaf litter if they weren't busy recycling all that waste? A pooter is an essential part of the mini-beast hunter's toolkit but be warned, if you suck on the wrong end you may be in for a mouth full of creepy crawlies!

A wildlife garden without water is like an orchard without fruit trees. Everyone needs a drink and some need a bath, too. In Chapter 3 meet the characters of a garden pond: the water boatmen, water slaters and azure damselflies. Discover who the hawkers, darters and chasers are, and how

The final chapter equips us with knowledge on some of the bigger issues affecting the wildlife gardener. Few of us garden in isolation so we need to know how our actions and those of our neighbours can be harnessed to boost biodiversity. In the face of the earth's Sixth Mass Extinction, could inspiring the Nature Deficit Disorder generation be the key to long-term species recovery?

So for answers to this and more, dip in for a five-minute eye-opener or read from cover-to-cover. *How Can I Help Hedgehogs?* demonstrates that we can all make a difference if we share a love of gardens and their wildlife.

Chapter 1

In the Air

How can I bring more small birds into the garden?

WHEN YOU'VE PUT A LOT OF effort into trying to cater for the birds that visit your garden, it can be frustrating if your plot seems to be monopolized by pigeons and the occasional magpie. It's great to have any birds share your space, but what's the best way to attract an even wider range, including some of the smaller birds such as robins, finches and tits?

Who likes what?

The days of a bird table featuring bread crusts and biscuit crumbs are long gone. There are dozens of different wild bird foods available commercially, from sunflower hearts (seeds with the skins already removed) to fat balls or bars incorporating nuts, seeds and dried fruit. Plenty of others, such as fresh or dried fruit, can come from your own supplies. You can even buy fresh mealworms for the insectivores. And there are feeders to match different styles, from hanging perches to tables and small-gauge cages.

Pigeon preferences

One of the reasons that pigeons are so ubiquitous is their unfussy feeding habits. Their natural diet consists of grains and seeds, but also green leaves and buds, and they will happily try any bird food you supply. Naturally, though, they are ground-feeders rather than perchers.

Of the other birds you might attract, robins, thrushes and sparrows also prefer to take food directly from the ground. For these birds, consider buying a ground feeder with a protective wire cover over it. The smaller birds will make their way

Research suggests there is a natural pecking order between different bird species at bird feeders, with heavier birds being dominant. If you want your garden to appeal to as many species as possible, look at the specifics of what they like – and at ways to thwart the pigeons from eating all the food before the smaller birds arrive.

Blue tits (*Cyanistes caerulus*) are agile users of hanging bird feeders and enjoy a wide variety of foods including nuts, seeds and suet balls.

through the bars easily, but pigeons won't be able to get through, so leave some food on the ground outside, too, so that they get their share. That way you ensure maximum garden diversity not so much by excluding the pigeons as by enabling the other species.

Hanging feeders can benefit birds other than pigeons and thwart

squirrels, too. A guardian (a protective wire cage) placed over the feeder works well to exclude squirrels and some of the larger birds, giving the smaller species a chance to feed. And many smaller birds such as finches and tits prefer feeders they can perch on. You can also hang fat balls and bars inside cages or, if you've grown your own sunflowers, a whole seed head can be suspended with a wire or string through its stem.

CAN SPARROWS STAGE A COMEBACK?

Huge drops in populations of house sparrows, as high as a 60 per cent fall in a 10-year period at the turn of the millennium, but levelling off since 2009, have been recorded in major cities all over the world, from London to Delhi. Many factors have been blamed, from pollution to food shortages. While a drop in the number of invertebrates that make up most of the sparrow chicks' diet is a problem, current thinking is that the major reason may be a lack of nesting sites. Sparrows like to nest in groups, so a number of nests may be constructed close

together. Traditionally favoured spots were under deep house eaves, in holes and corners in masonry and inside hedges and large shrubs, all of which are becoming less common in towns. If you can find a suitable spot on a wall or under eaves, you can help by setting up a row of communal nest boxes. Add a consistent supply of food and you may find that you've gained your own family of sparrows. Breeding pairs can produce up to four broods a year.

Sparrows aren't territorial and often nest very close together; they're usually quick to occupy nest boxes if they're offered.

Why do butterflies love buddleia?

NOT FOR NOTHING is buddleia called the 'butterfly bush'; *Buddleja davidii*, to give it its full botanical name, flowers even in unpromising circumstances, and can be seen everywhere from railway embankments, where it copes well on poor soil, to upmarket gardens, where the latest cultivar may be showcased. What, though, makes it quite so attractive to butterflies?

The long tubular-shaped flowers of buddleias are perfectly adapted to the long proboscis (tongue) of butterflies and the large flowerheads allow them to perch as they feed. Buddleias flower prolifically, most over a long season, and are both heavily scented and full of nectar: where butterflies are concerned, what's not to like?

All-round appeal

Butterflies aren't the buddleias' only fans: many moths and bees are enthusiastic about them, too. But buddleia isn't even a European native. It actually hails from China, although its name comes, more prosaically, from the Reverend Adam Buddle, a 17th-century Essex vicar.

Keep a balanced environment

Even if your garden is a small one, ecologists urge you to keep the all-round picture in mind when you plant. A 30-year study at a garden in Leicestershire discovered 19 species of moth caterpillar feeding on buddleia. It does not, however, seem to be so attractive to butterfly caterpillars, so to be certain that your garden provides for all stages of a butterfly's life cycle it is good to incorporate at least some plants that are known to nourish their caterpillars.

A separate book could be written on who likes what. The notorious cabbage white lays waste to your brassicas, orange tip and green-veined white butterflies favour lady's smock

BEST BUDDLEIAS FOR BUTTERFLIES

A line-up of the top five cultivars, selected from the National Plant Collection at Longstock Park Nursery in Hampshire, where Peter Moore, who manages the collection, says that the level of butterfly attraction depends on the nectar quality rather than the appearance of the flower.

Painted lady,
Vanessa cardui

Buddleja davidii '**Autumn Delight**' Pinkish red flowers, especially attractive to butterflies such as peacocks and tortoiseshells later in the season. Height 200–300cm (80–120in), spread 200cm (80in).

Buddleja × weyeriana '**Pink Pagoda**' (PBR) This weyeriana hybrid has clean pink flower spires, each flower with a bright orange eye. Attractive to bees and butterflies. Height 150–300cm (60–120in) high, spread 150cm (60in).

Buddleja [Sugar Plum] '**Lonplum**' (PBR) A rich, deep pinkish-red with long, tapering blooms. Appeals to many varieties of both butterfly and moth. Height (relatively compact) 150cm (60in), spread 150cm (60in).

Buddleja davidii '**Summer House Blue**' Pale, china-blue flowers with silvery leaves. Attractive to various species, including painted lady. Height 150–200cm, (60–80in) spread 150cm (60in).

Buddleja davidii '**White Profusion**' (right) A large buddleia with profuse white flowers, each with a yellow eye. Appeals to a number of butterflies, including red admirals and peacocks. Height >250cm (100in), spread >250cm (100in).

(*Cardamine pratensis*) or garlic mustard (*Alliaria petiolata*), commas like golden hop (*Humulus lupulus* 'Aureus'), and both holly and ivy play host to holly blues. Outside your garden, buddleias can actually prove to be an invasive weed, for example in chalk grassland, where they tend to colonize areas that would otherwise be useful habitat for a whole range of rare invertebrates.

Which flowers are friendliest for moths?

MOSTLY NIGHT-FLYING, moths tend to be seen as less glamorous than butterflies. But moths are far more numerous, more likely to breed in your garden and, viewed up close and personal, they are just as interesting and even more varied. There are also some stunning and colourful day-flying species. So it's worth taking their tastes into consideration when you're choosing plants.

Small elephant hawk-moth, *Deilephila porcellus*

Adult moths drink nectar and most are nocturnal, so pale flowers with a strong night scent tend to be the best choices. That said, the huge moth family has plenty of specialists who will enjoy very specific plants.

Moth lives

Moth species make up 96 per cent of the group Lepidoptera, which they share with butterflies – over 150,000 species have been identified globally, with more being added all the time. With so many to record, moth specialists have made two broad divisions: macro- and micro-. Mainly this is just an indication of size (though, confusingly, some of the largest micro-moths are bigger than the smallest macro- types). Moths don't have the mouthparts for eating; they can only drink, using the curved tube

of a proboscis to suck up nectar. Some shorter-lived species don't feed at all as adults, eating only at their caterpillar stage, so if you want the greatest range possible, it's worth paying attention to their larval plant preferences, too.

Daytime stars

Every year there are a few reported sightings of hummingbirds in UK gardens. What observers have really seen is the hummingbird hawk-moth (*Macroglossum stellatarum*). A migrant from Southern Europe, it's a day-flying moth with a wingspan of up to 5.8cm (2 1/4in), which hovers, appearing almost motionless, around its favourite food plants, including buddleia and red valerian. Also relatively common in the UK and Europe is its equally large and sensationally colourful relative, the elephant hawk-moth (*Deilephila elpenor*), which has bright pink stripes on its wings and body against an olive background. Its large caterpillars – which can grow up to

8cm (3in) long – munch on fuchsia and rose bay willowherb.

At the smaller end of the scale is the mint moth (*Pyrausta aurata*), a brown moth with pretty, subtle markings, who both feeds and breeds in the herb garden, frequenting not only mint but many other herbs, including marjoram and oregano. It's a good reminder that a herb patch isn't just useful for the kitchen: it's great for moths and butterflies, too.

PLANTS MOTHS LOVE

Moths favour nectar-rich plants; these are five of their top picks. Aim to grow a range of moth-friendly plants that stay in flower across as long a season as possible.

Red campion (*Silene dioica*) The campions (right) are all-round wildlife magnets, and the red campion is popular with moths, hoverflies and bumblebees. It self-seeds lavishly, so you may need to keep it in check, but its appeal to insects makes it worth it.

Tobacco plants (*Nicotiana alata*) The original form of the popular trumpet-flowered bedding plant. Seek out and grow from seed, as modern varieties sometimes aren't as rich in either scent or nectar, and in some cases the 'trumpet' has become so elongated that the moths' tongues can't reach the nectar.

Night-scented stock (*Matthiola longipetala* subsp. *bicormis*) Easy-to-grow annual with simple lilac, white or pink flowers. Both people and moths enjoy the heady nocturnal scent.

Red valerian (*Centranthus ruber*) An easy-care perennial (left) with clusters of small pink, trumpet-shaped flowers and a long flowering season, starting in April and lasting until at least August or, if it's cut back judiciously in July, even longer.

Where's best for a bird box?

IF YOU'VE ENCOURAGED more bird species into your garden
by feeding them, the next step is to see if you can get them to stay
and nest. With wildlife gardening becoming fashionable, there's
a bewildering variety of artificial nest boxes available, from basic
boxes to elaborate designs in novelty shapes and wine-gum colours.
Which is best, which species will it suit and where should it be sited?

Birds looking for a nesting
spot won't care about how
stylish a potential home looks:
the right des res will be well
sited, secure and weatherproof.
The best box design and
position will depend on which
birds you're hoping to attract.

Who likes which box?

Unless you've often seen them
around your garden or it borders onto
a different sort of habitat such as
farmland or woodland, it's best not to
set your heart on rarities with very

specific needs, such as owls or swallows.
Some species are far more widespread
and also more likely to use ready-made
accommodation than others. Boxes with
the highest success rate in gardens are
usually those aimed at robins and blue
tits, though that doesn't mean you won't
attract something rarer or less expected.
Time-wise, you should put the boxes up
in autumn or winter, so that they're all
ready when birds' thoughts turn to
nesting in early spring.

Must-haves (and have-nots)

Boxes should be made of untreated
timber or, better, a material called
woodcrete (made from a mix of sawdust
and concrete). Woodcrete is very sturdy
with good insulation, so these boxes
stay warm when it's cold outside and
cool when it's hot. The two main styles
of box either have an entrance hole or
are open-fronted: the latter is more
likely to be used by robins, spotted
flycatchers and blackbirds but leaves
chicks very vulnerable to predators, so
extra care should be taken when siting
them. The size of the entrance hole
affects who will use the box: smaller

POINTS TO REMEMBER WHEN POSITIONING A BIRD BOX

- Site boxes with entrance holes around 1.5 to 2m (4 to 6ft) up, on a fence, wall or tree in a quietish part of your garden.

- Situate boxes well away from your bird feeders.

- If your box is to be fixed on a tree trunk, don't nail or screw it in place as this may injure the tree. Instead, use cable ties or rubber-coated cable.

- Face wooden boxes between north-east and south-east (use a compass to check). If they face into full sun, they will get too hot. Woodcrete can go in a sunnier spot as it regulates temperature better.

- Avoid spots with nearby branches, offering easy 'reach' for cats or squirrels.

- Boxes with entrance holes are best hung with an open approach. Place open-fronted boxes next to plenty of surrounding foliage (on a wall behind a dense climber, for example) for protection.

▲ Male wrens (*Troglodytes troglodytes*) are strongly territorial and may build several nests – sometimes taking advantage of nesting boxes – in the hope of tempting a female into one of them.

entrances will suit blue tits, for example; slightly larger ones will fit great tits or even woodpeckers. Boxes should also have a hinged top lid or other form of access, so that you can clean them out when the nesting season is over. Fit a metal nest box protection plate to stop predators enlarging the hole.

There are a couple of other tips: don't pick a box with a perch under the entrance hole – they're handy for predators such as grey squirrels to balance on while they try to get access to the nestlings. And don't choose one of the combined feeder-and-nest box units that you may see on sale, because nesting birds will feel threatened by the proximity of others feeding and the box is unlikely to find any takers.

Are any insects really pests?

If, as a gardener, you've absorbed the diversity message, you might wonder if any invertebrates should be unwelcome in your garden, even when your tolerance is tested in years that are particularly successful for slugs or aphids. What's the best policy for invertebrates: should you maintain a multiple-legs-good approach?

Know your invertebrates

Most habitats, even very small ones, support a complex web of creatures, delicately balanced. If you classify invertebrates by their diet and role, you'll find there are herbivores, detritivores, predators and omnivores. The first group eat plants; the second, decomposing matter, whether animal or vegetable; the third eat other invertebrates; and the fourth and final group dine on a wider range, including both plants and other invertebrates. If a resource, perhaps a food source or a living space, for one or more species becomes scarce, that species will suffer; conversely, if resources for one or

more species become more readily available, those species will multiply more successfully. Over time, if the environment remains generally diverse, the balance will usually return, sometimes through a series of knock-on effects. More food for one species may lead its numbers to increase, but as its numbers increase, there may not be enough food for the increased population, or its natural predators may also boom, for instance. The other thing that may cause a species imbalance is unbalanced planting. If one or two species of

▼ Aphids secrete a sweet liquid that ants enjoy, but to numerous other species they're a valued food item in their own right.

Diversity and balance are key. It's usually only when a natural balance is upset and one species gains a notable advantage that the resulting population explosion leads gardeners to see it as a pest. Sometimes this happens because of human interference, but sometimes over-population arises naturally.

plant that appeal only to a few sorts of invertebrate start to take over in a garden, numbers of those invertebrates will increase (and there'll be a drop in those species for which that particular plant doesn't offer food or shelter). This is one of the reasons why modern farming, with its large areas of single crops, tends not to encourage diversity. Even where farming is done without pesticides, the single-note nature of farmed crops will only suit a very limited range of wildlife.

From the wildlife gardener's point of view, some insects may at times be irritants, but they shouldn't really ever be regarded as pests.

Slugs and snails famously love hostas. For the wildlife gardener, it makes more sense to protect the plants (perhaps growing them in pots) than to kill the so-called pests.

WHEN THE BALANCE IS UPSET

Every so often, a very cold winter followed by an extra-warm spring will herald an explosion of aphids, and their natural predators – such as ladybirds and their larvae, certain hoverfly larvae, earwigs and lacewings – while feeding rapidly, are overwhelmed by the endless supply. This overload, though it may be unpopular with gardeners, is likely to have a knock-on effect: later in the year or the following year, aphid predators will enjoy their own upturn having benefitted from an aphid-rich diet and produced more young than usual as a result.

If you have a 'pest' year, remember just how important invertebrates are, not only in the overall natural scheme of things, but for the human race specifically: among a host of services, they filter our water, they maintain links in the food web and they ensure the survival of many of our crops. The eminent US biologist E O Wilson put it in these terms: 'If human beings were to disappear tomorrow, the world would go on with little change. But if invertebrates were to vanish, I doubt that the human species would last more than a few months.'

How does a lawn become a wildflower meadow?

WILDFLOWER MEADOWS are constantly cited as being great for wildlife. If you already have a lawn, how easy would it be to turn it into a meadow and what work is involved?

Annual vs. perennial

Most gardens have comparatively rich soil, in which case an annual flower mix may be the easiest option. These need bare soil to germinate. The classic are 'cornfield' annuals, usually a mix of corn marigold, corn cockle, cornflower, corn chamomile and corn poppy, which will attract plenty of insects and may self-seed to some extent. A perennial meadow is a mix of wildflowers and grasses: in nature, they thrive on poor soil, because it keeps balance between the two. Rich soil may mean that the grass grows strongly and overwhelms the flowers, so only lawns on poor soils or where no fertilizers have been added are suitable for conversion.

▼ Most annual 'meadow' flower mixes give you a colourful result including, among other annuals, bright red corn poppies and vivid blue cornflowers.

Working with what you have

If your garden has poor soil, you can probably turn your lawn into a perennial meadow. It will take around three years to complete the transformation. You begin with a simple regime of neglect: mow the grass once a week, collect the clippings, but don't weed or fertilize. A year in, start to let the grass grow. Some wildlife-friendly flowers such as clover, buttercup and dandelion will start to appear; leave them to set seed and plant new flowers such as ox-eye daisy, greater knapweed and meadow clary in small groups, either as small plug plants or grown from seed. At the end of the second year, mow after the flowers have gone to seed, once again collecting the grass clippings, then mow once a year, only after the plants

have gone to seed. Planting yellow rattle will help reduce the vigour of grass if it is still too thuggish.

Making a meadow from scratch

If you decide on an annual mix or want to grow a wildflower perennial meadow from seed, it's best done in early spring. If you're planning a small area, the turf can be stripped off with a spade and dug over by hand, but for a larger area, you may need to use a mechanical turf stripper and rotovator. Rake over the soil, leave it for six weeks, then weed before sowing. Wildflower meadows can also be sown in autumn. There is quite a wide choice of 'meadow' seed mixes; choose one that suits your garden conditions and decide whether you want indigenous

A To create a true perennial meadow will take some time, but all lawns can be enriched for wildlife; how much work it will involve depends on the kind (and size) of lawn you have already and whether you want flowers only or a mix of flowers and grass. In some cases you can work with what you've got; in others, you'll need to prepare the ground before sowing.

plants only, or a wider mix that includes non-natives. Seed sowing rates for meadows are very low, so mix the seed with a little silver sand, so you can see clearly where you've sown and where you still have to cover.

MADE FOR MEADOWS: YELLOW RATTLE

It's attractive in its own right, with stalks of bee-friendly flowers standing bolt upright in high summer, but yellow rattle (*Rhinanthus minor*) can also be a help in establishing a wildflower meadow. As a semi-parasite it suppresses meadow grasses, ensuring that some soil resources are left for other flowering plants to benefit. The 'parasite' part means that the rattle's roots entwine with the roots of grasses and suck nutrients from them, reducing their vigour; the 'semi' part means that, unlike a fully parasitic plant, yellow rattle also produces a proportion of its own food through photosynthesis. It's a vigorous self-seeder – once introduced to grassland, it tends to persist and establish itself. If you're creating a meadow, ensure that the mix you choose includes yellow rattle; in an established meadow, sow fresh seed on pre-scarified areas in autumn.

Who's biting through my flowers at the stem end?

Y OU PROBABLY THINK you know how pollination works: a bee or other insect visits a flower to collect nectar and pollen, picks up some extra pollen along the way, then flies off to another flower where it inadvertently deposits pollen on the stigma, kicking off the whole floral fertilization process. That's one part of the narrative, but it's far from the whole story.

Blue carpenter bee, *Xylocopa violacea*

Tricky trumpet flowers

Open-faced flowers are a free-for-all when it comes to nectar collection. But plants with deeper, trumpet-shaped or hooded blooms – think of salvias, for example, or broad beans – pose a challenge to insects who don't have long tongues. Short-tongued bee species, such as the buff-tailed bumblebee and carpenter bee, have learned that biting through the base of the hood of such deep flowers can earn them a quick fix of nectar without the difficulties (or in some cases, the flat impossibility) of working themselves into the flower and taking the nectar in the conventional way.

There are lots of species of bee (over 270 species in the UK) and their body size and tongue length will largely determine whether they can reach inside a flower to get to the nectar. Those little holes in your flowers are a sign that a particular bee failed to reach the nectar by conventional means and had to resort to robbing nectar instead.

Flowers fight back

A study published by Kew Gardens in 2017 showed that there's evidence that some flowers have learned to resist the nectar robbing by producing unpalatable nectar. The study found examples of monkshood (*Aconitum*) plants, with hooded, tubular flowers,

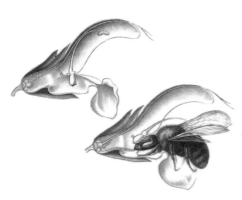

◀ Long-tongued bee species find it easier to reach the nectar in deep flowers such as this clary sage (*Salvia sclarea*) bloom.

which had notably fewer short-tongued bee visitors. When analyzed, those flowers' nectar had higher levels of an alkaloid, aconitine, which seemed to make it less palatable to insects. Long-tongued bees, once in the flower, took the nectar anyway (and also pollinated the plant); short-tongued bees seemed to sense that it wasn't worth boring into the flower to steal. Scientists speculated that the long-tongued bees had developed a greater tolerance to the aconitine, while the short-tongued bees, which were not nectar specialists, had decided that the flowers weren't worth their effort.

Can you stop nectar robbers?

What's the gardener's takeaway from these bee stories? There's no effective way to stop nectar robbers (and they don't really harm your enjoyment of your flowers, although affected crops such as broad bean may take longer to set beans). So it's best to be generous and try to ensure that your garden offers something for everybody in the pollinator world. A full buffet of nectar possibilities means planting plenty of flowers of different structures: open, trumpet and everything in between.

BUZZ POLLINATION

Sometimes an insect takes advantage of a flower; sometimes, though, a flower has evolved to take advantage of an insect. And that's what happens with buzz pollination. Pollen is costly for a flower to produce, taking up lots of resources. Some flowers, despite this, are quite profligate with their pollen: an insect brushes against the anther and pollen rubs off. Others have so-called poricidal anthers, with pollen concealed in tube-like structures, offering no chance of casual pollination.

To get the job done, they need 'buzz pollination', also called sonication. Tomato is a good example of a plant requiring 'buzz pollination'. A bee lands on the flower, then holds still and vibrates its wing muscles to produce a strong buzz at a specific frequency. At a certain point, the poricidal anther responds to this by releasing a pay-off explosion of pollen. The majority of these flowers don't offer nectar as well: the pollen, which is a major protein source for the insect's young, is the bee's reward for its efforts. The plant's reward is that the bee, now liberally covered with pollen, will go off to visit another plant of the same type and have a high pollination success rate.

Can I make my garden bat-friendly?

BATS ARE SOME OF THE MORE ELUSIVE ANIMALS you can attract to your garden, and whether or not they visit – or even roost – may depend to some extent on your proximity to other bat-friendly habitats. But with 45 species of bat across Europe, 18 of which are found in the UK, it's well worth trying a number of simple ways to raise your garden's bat appeal.

Daubenton's bat,
Myotis daubentonii

Night dining

Bats eat a wide range of nocturnal insects, mostly on the wing. The easiest way to attract a feast for a bat is to grow as broad a selection as possible of night-scented flowers: what's good for moths and other night-fliers is going to be good for bats. If you can also offer a pond, bats will not only drink from it but may also hunt the midges, mosquitoes and other insects around it. Daubenton's bat (*Myotis daubentonii*) in particular is an enthusiast for water; it uses its large feet and mobile tail to sweep up insects and larvae from the pond's surface. The bats you're most likely to see in a UK garden are one or more of the three species of pipistrelles (*Pipistrellus pipistrellus*, *P. nathusii* and *P. pygmaeus*): minute bats weighing just 5g, which have an irregular flitting flight pattern as they pursue their insect prey. Other possible sightings could be of the much larger – starling-sized – noctule (*Nyctalus noctula*), which flies in a straight line with sudden dips as it swoops on insects or, if you live near woodland, the brown long-eared bat (*Plecotus auritus*), which tends to stick near to trees and can be identified by its fluttering flight, weaving between the branches.

Bat lifestyles

Bats spend at least three months of the year hibernating, usually in groups, in a quiet, cool roost which they will have sought out in late autumn. They begin to reappear in February or early March, as the fat stores they built up pre-hibernation begin to run low. By April they will be out hunting most nights and will be roosting in new, warmer spots during the day. By late spring,

Bats aren't as predictable as many other species, but if you can lay on a regular supply of their preferred food, plus some quiet, dark corners without any lighting in the vicinity, you'll increase your chances not only of seeing them but also of attracting them to roost.

the sexes are roosting separately, as the females prepare to give birth to their single offspring, called a pup. Young bats will feed on their mother's milk for about six weeks before they start to hunt independently. Once their pups are off their hands, females begin to mix with males and will choose mating roosts where they will spend the daylight hours. Bats mate in autumn and both sexes begin to build up their fat stores in preparation for going back into hibernation. The females are pregnant during the hibernation months.

Roosting options

From this cycle you can see that bats have several types of roost: a hibernation roost, a maternity roost and mating roosts where males and females mix. Many choose trees to roost in, using spaces behind the bark or spots deep in the forks of branches. Others roost in buildings, in quiet spaces under the eaves or in the roof; they do no damage and should not be disturbed.

OFFERING A BAT BOX

Bat boxes are quite differently shaped from bird boxes, with a flat, stepped shape and narrow entry slots. If you'd like to try one in your garden, choose a sunny site at least 4m (13ft) up on a wall or tree... and wait. Bats often take their time with a new site, so it may be a long-term project, but keep an eye on it, and after two or three years, you may be lucky. And when bats have occupied a roost, they tend to return to it in successive years. You can't disturb a box once its inhabited, so look out for the signs: dry bat droppings on the landing area and below the box and possibly small 'chatty' noises on a warm day.

Why are single flowers better?

FLOWERING PLANTS NEED INSECTS to pollinate them and evolved in shapes that made the job easy. The pollinating insect would head for the nectar and would encounter the pollen, heavy and sticky, on its way, making it inevitable that it would carry some grains on to the next flower. Modern ornamentals, though, aren't always bred with the insect's interests in mind.

Complicated ornamentals with double petals, elaborate 'closed' shapes and lower fragrance levels are all less attractive to pollinating insects than open, easy-access flowers. And some hybrids have no pollen at all, having been bred for single-generation flowering, not for seeds.

Shapes and structures

You might think the ideal flower for a pollinating insect, therefore, is something like a primrose or a foxglove. But there are plenty of other options, including composite flowers, in which a single inflorescence may comprise multiple tiny flowers on the same flower head, such as a sunflower or lawn daisy, for example.

Blue daisy,
Felicia amelloides

FALSE ADVERTISING

Flowers cost a lot of energy for plants to produce, so some plants have evolved to take a shortcut: they produce 'false' sterile flowers (sepals that have acquired the visual 'advertising' of flowers) which give a shout-out to pollinating insects that they're worth visiting, and which surround much smaller, fertile real flowers that actually produce the nectar and pollen. Wild hydrangea heads, for example, have a small centre of fertile flowers with an outer circle of showy sterile 'flowers' to draw the pollinators in, and they're popular with a wide range of insects. However, many hydrangea cultivars have been bred for the showy aspect: not much use to pollinators, as the sterile element far outweighs the fertile one.

Is garden lighting disruptive?

GARDEN LIGHTING IS A POPULAR WAY to extend the visual appeal of your garden after dark. But does it disrupt the natural cycles of the wildlife you've spent time assiduously encouraging? And are some types of lighting better than others?

Most research into light pollution shows that it has an adverse effect on a wide range of species, so ideally your garden shouldn't be lit. If you really want light in a specific spot, limit its use and ensure there are other areas of the garden that are dark all night.

A lighter world

Our world has got brighter. And although there's still much research to be done, it's known that most of the wildlife around us takes cues from the light levels, so perpetual light can confuse nocturnal species (moths and other species navigate by natural light such as the moon so strong artificial light disorientates them), mislead birds (which have been recorded singing in the middle of the night in strongly lit areas) and stress trees, which may respond to near-perpetual light by producing oversized foliage or even altering their flowering season. Some species, notably amphibians, are attracted to light, too, while others, including certain bat species, seem to try to avoid lit areas altogether.

Lighting rules

If possible, avoid lighting your garden: if you're eating al fresco after dark, for example, rediscover candlelight, rather than installing artificial lights. If you must have lights, some seem to impact wildlife less than others: there's evidence that softer amber lights are less disruptive than the unfiltered blue or white light of LED (light-emitting diode) bulbs. Similarly, less light is lost to the night sky with downlighting than uplighting, reducing light pollution. If you really need to install a security light, choose the kind triggered by movement rather than one that's on all the time. Finally, it's best not to light a water feature or pond: the water-dependent species can't simply move away from any unwelcome glare.

Why should I welcome wasps?

THE INSECT YOU IMMEDIATELY THINK OF when you hear the word 'wasp' is *Vespula vulgaris*, the boldly striped common wasp, ubiquitous in most gardens in late summer, buzzing around your windfalls and dive-bombing your picnics. But this is only one of an estimated 9,000 wasp species in the UK, most of which play important roles in your garden's ecosystem.

Which wasp?

Wasps divide into two broad types: social and solitary. The common wasp is one of just seven social species that live in the UK, each of which lives in its own community. Common wasps occupy an exquisite papier-mâché-like nest made by wasp workers from fragments of chewed wood. Social wasps have a set-up somewhat like that of honeybees: they live in colonies with a queen to create her eggs and numerous workers to feed and care for them. The colonies last for only a year, from spring to autumn, when the colder weather arrives. Young queens (called gynes) will find shelter to overwinter, then start up fresh colonies in spring.

In the insect food web, common wasps are what's known as apex predators; they perch at the top of the garden insect food chain, consuming huge numbers of greenfly, caterpillars and flies. Overall, the common wasp and other members of this vast family are garden friends, not foes, and a healthy wasp population tends to indicate that all is well in the garden.

Family life

Unlike bees, wasps feed their larvae on smaller insects and other prey – hence their value as predators – so when they visit flowers it is to take care of their own food needs, not those of their young. The adults live only a few months and sustain themselves with nectar, and it's in the course

◀ The common wasp (*Vespula vulgaris*) has a largely undeserved reputation for aggression; if left alone, it doesn't usually sting.

of gathering it that they add to their all-round value by multitasking as pollinators.

Picnic pests

In the nest, each wasp larva 'rewards' an adult who arrives with food by exuding a drop of a sugary liquid for it to eat. The reason that wasps have a tendency to buzz around sugary drinks and food in late summer is that, when their colony has grown, there are fewer and fewer larvae; starved of their sugar fix, they start to look for it elsewhere.

The parasitoid lifestyle

As well as the social species, there's a huge number of different kinds of solitary wasp, whose females live single and very diverse lives. Solitary wasps differ widely in size, from those so tiny that they can eat an aphid from the inside out all the way up to the sabre wasp (*Rhyssa persuasoria*), which can grow 4cm (1$\frac{1}{2}$in) long. Most solitary wasps are elegant ichneumonids, with long antennae, exaggerated 'wasp' waists and, in the case of females, long, curving ovipositors, from which they lay their eggs, at the end of the abdomen.

The vast majority of ichneumonids are parasitoid. In their egg and larval stages they live on, or in, a host who, in the course of their development, they will kill and eat. In most cases, the ovipositor will be used to lay an egg or eggs into the living body of a caterpillar or a spider, or even another

species of wasp or bee (each type has its species preference); when the egg hatches, the larva will eat up its host from within. Ichneumonids are widespread in garden habitats; once you're familiar with their looks, you'll find the larger species easy to spot.

WHAT ABOUT HORNETS?

At around 3.5cm (1$\frac{1}{3}$in) an adult queen is big enough to scare the most resolute gardener, but the European hornet (*Vespa crabro*) doesn't sting unless really pushed. It's calmer than some of the other social species. If you see one (it looks like a large common wasp but with brown-and-gold stripes), admire its impressive size from a distance and bear in mind that the species is in decline. In some European countries, it's illegal to harm one; certainly don't kill it.

European hornet,
Vespa crabro

Should I have a bee hotel?

THEY'VE BECOME POPULAR PROJECTS for gardens and are often used as a way to teach children about wildlife. And made and maintained properly, bee hotels can be a great way to offer nest sites for solitary bees. But it's worth finding out about your potential tenants, and learning how to be a responsible landlord, before you either make or buy one.

Although the terms 'bug hotel' and 'bee hotel' have come to be used almost interchangeably, most potential users – from bees to lacewings to ladybirds – have very specific needs when it comes to nesting. If you want to become a bee hotelier, do a little research first.

What makes a good hotel?

The idea behind a bee hotel is that it provides ready-made accommodation for solitary bees looking for a place to nest. The broader term 'bug hotel' implies homes for many different invertebrates from beetles to bees but not

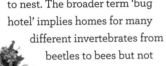

all insects will like the same conditions, so it's best to aim to attract specific species and ensure their needs are met.

Mason and leafcutter bees are small, dark or ginger bees with yellow undercarriages and make good candidates for a hotel. In spring and early summer, they seek out tunnels to nest in. Leafcutter bees line them with neat leaf segments, while mason bees favour a mud lining. When the nest is made the bee will lay an egg or eggs, leave a supply of pollen, seal it up and leave. The eggs hatch into larvae which will complete their transformation into bees and emerge around 11 months later. You may spot bees coming in and out during the nesting stage and a tunnel sealed with leaves or mud indicates a bee has laid its eggs there.

Bee tunnels need to be warm and dry. Some of the commercially available versions feature Perspex or thick cardboard tunnels, but Perspex can end up with condensation inside, which may rot the eggs or larvae, and cardboard can become damp. Wood or bamboo are the best materials.

SETTING UP A BEE HOTEL

If you'd like to make your own bee hotel, it's easy to do. Remember that you should only use untreated wood.

1 For the most basic model, drill a block of untreated wood with a series of holes 7–10mm (c2/5in) in diameter. Red mason bees are likely to use holes 7–8mm (^{1}/4in) in diameter, leafcutter bees the larger holes. They should be the depth of a drill bit (bees nest in closed-end tunnels) and should be smooth and emptied of sawdust. Then fix the block in the site you've chosen, which should be a warm, sunny, open spot 1–1.5m (3–4ft) off the ground.

2 A more complex version can be made by nailing together a box around 2–5cm deep, with a roof that overhangs to offer shelter from rain. Add a back, so that it's kept dry.

3 Take a number of wooden blocks or sections of tree branch or bamboo, cut them to the depth of the box, then drill them with holes, as above, and stack them end-on in the box with the open end of each tunnel at the front.

Red mason bee,
Osmia bicornis

4 Hang the box securely on a suitable fence or wall.

5 Keep an eye on the hotel: you may see bees arriving to check it out and if the mouths of some of the holes have been blocked, it means that eggs have been laid and in due course larvae should hatch out.

6 Remember maintenance. Any tunnels that are still sealed by the following autumn indicate that a bee laid eggs but either they didn't hatch, or the larvae didn't reach adulthood successfully, so the holes should be cleaned out for another resident. Blocks should be replaced every third year.

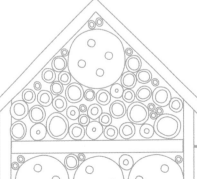

Should I keep honeybees?

YOU MIGHT ASSUME that anything that increases the honeybee population has to be a good thing. But recent studies have called into question whether the current explosion of 'hobby' hives in certain built-up areas is doing the overall bee population much good.

It's a difficult question: honeybees are under threat, but no more so than the thousands of species of wild bees, which are arguably even more important. If you're committed to maintaining diverse bee life, it's probably best to concentrate on helping the wild bees.

It's complicated

There are around 270 bee species in the UK and an estimated 2,000 across Europe, and that's out of what is believed to be about 10,000 species worldwide. The honeybee is only one of them, and all bees have evolved to fit with their surroundings and can be extremely specialized feeders and pollinators.

Wild vs. 'managed' bees

At the same time that beekeeping is seeing a resurgence in popularity as a hobby, habitat that is rich in diverse plants and flowers is dwindling, so it's inevitable that bee species will be in competition with one another. A range of studies internationally, including one published by Cambridge University in 2018, concluded that farmed bees aren't helpful to wild species. In addition to the problem of limited resources, bees also spread pathogens as they collect nectar and pollinate. If a colony of honeybees, with anything up to 60,000 members, is sick, that's a lot of potential infection to pass on to wild species who may not have much resistance. So if you want to help all bees, look at ways you can ensure your garden appeals to the maximum number of different bee species. If you'd really love to have your own hive, contact your local beekeeping society, learn as much as you can about beekeeping and ask plenty of questions about how rich the local foraging habitat is for all bee species before you take the plunge.

Is a butterfly feeder a good idea?

WITH THE INCREASING POPULARITY of wildlife gardens, there are both commercial and home-made options for feeding almost every insect or animal you can imagine. You already have a bird table and feeders, so is it worth trying out the butterfly equivalent?

A natural diet

Butterflies don't have the mouthparts to eat solids; instead, they nourish themselves by sucking up flower nectar through the proboscis, a long, curled tube that works like a straw (a few, short-lived species don't feed as adults at all, taking in a life's worth of nutrition at the larval, caterpillar, stage). Some species will also feed on the sweet juices of overripe fruit. There isn't much evidence that setting up feeding stations for butterflies is helpful; instead, look at finding flowering plants that will give them the longest possible season to feed naturally. This may mean planting a mixture of natives, such as red clover and St John's wort, and cultivated plants that will offer plenty of nectar and may extend the season during which butterflies can feed, such as veronicas, hebes, echinacea, buddleia and single-flowered dahlias.

Purple
coneflower,
*Echinacea
purpurea*

Red clover,
Trifolium pratense

The idea of a butterfly feeder is often presented as a craft project, sometimes one to make with children. This might be a fun activity but from the wildlife's point of view, it's better to concentrate on growing the broadest range of nectar-laden flowers you can.

Can I help with nesting material?

DIFFERENT BIRD SPECIES use a big range of materials to make their nests. Can you help them out by supplying them with some useful ingredients? And are there any materials that you should avoid offering altogether?

Take two nests

Just a couple of examples will give you an idea of the different approaches to nest building of different species. At the casual end of the scale is the wood pigeon's (*Columba palumbus*) nest. These are made quite roughly from twigs and are shaped as an open platform. They don't take very long to

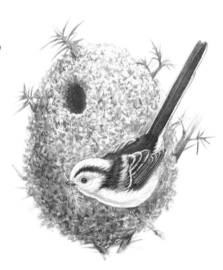

The long-tailed tit (*Aegithalos caudatus*) builds a nest that not only has a neatly domed roof but is also slightly elastic due to its spiderweb 'mortar'.

build, and empty nests are often easy to spot in winter when the trees and tall shrubs that house them are bare of leaves. Wood pigeons spend more time breeding than building: each pair will raise between one and three broods of one or two chicks each over the breeding season.

At the elaborate end is the long-tailed tit; breeding pairs create an exquisite little construction with a small entrance hole near the top and a rounded belly to accommodate the forthcoming brood. The nest will usually be sited in the fork of a tree

Wood pigeons' nests are open, platform-like structures and their broods are small: the female lays only two eggs.

A From very simple constructions of stacked twigs to virtuoso masterpieces of moss, leaves and feathers, birds' nests are put together in plenty of different ways. And some offerings – combings of pet hair as long as it's chemical free, for example – will have a strong appeal to the right visitor.

a nesting spiral, usually sold either ready-packed with a range of materials from wool to grasses, or with small packs of sheep's wool or other ingredients ready to be filled.

Birds will select the materials that suit their particular nesting style. If you're putting out your own collection, avoid anything that has been chemically treated or processed. And hang up your feeder or spiral somewhere where you can enjoy watching the birds choose their pieces.

or deep in a hedge and is hard to spot; beautifully camouflaged, it's made from a patchwork of moss and lichen, welded together with pieces of spiderweb. When the outside is complete, a lining made from hundreds or even thousands of found feathers is added. Long-tailed tits raise a single annual brood, but it's a large one: anything from 8 to 15 chicks. And other longtails may help with feeding the family if they haven't managed a successful brood of their own.

What to offer

If you'd like to help with potentially useful nesting materials, all of the following are usually acceptable across a variety of species: combed-out chemical-free pet fur, or human hair; bits of leftover moss or straw from craft projects, sheep's wool or feathers, short lengths (no longer than 8cm/3in) of wool or natural-fibre string, and shredded paper. Pack the offerings loosely into a wire bird feeder or buy

NESTS WITH PESTS

Even if the material that you supply fits in naturally with birds' nest-building habits, there's evidence that birds will also customize their ingredients according to different needs. One study in Mexico City in 2012 found that house sparrows and finches were introducing the fibres from the filters of cigarette butts into nests that were infested with parasitic mites. The parasites didn't like the residual nicotine in the butts; if the nest didn't have any signs of past mite infestation, the cigarette filters hadn't been brought in. Possibly a case of meticulous avian housekeeping.

What is the 'dawn chorus'?

IF YOU'RE UP EARLY ENOUGH on a spring or summer morning between March and July, and you can open a window or get yourself outside somewhere where there are surrounding trees and greenery, you'll be rewarded by the sequence of birdsong called the dawn chorus. Why are the birds singing so early and what is the song for?

Song Thrush,
Turdus philomelos

Starting around an hour before dawn and usually lasting for up to an hour after it, the songs of the male birds that make up the dawn chorus signal their search for a mate and are also used to establish and defend breeding territory.

The morning concert

The chorus can still be quite noisy in areas where a variety of songbirds are living successfully with plenty of food and shelter. There's a rough order of service: first to sing are usually the thrushes, blackbirds and robins, followed by wood pigeons, warblers and wrens, and succeeded by the sparrows and great and blue tits. Studies have shown that the species with the largest eyes take the lead: bigger eyes have more adjustable pupils and can see better in low light, which may lead to the birds feeling safer in dim surroundings.

Why so early?

Very early morning is too dark for successful food foraging and songbirds out and about that early may also be more at risk from predators in the low light. So singing to attract a mate is a timely activity and, traditionally, the bird with the best voice wins a partner. A noisy, energetic song shows that the

Blackbird,
Turdus merula

bird it's issuing from is in good shape and is also likely to be a winning bet when it comes to breeding. As the year goes on and birds find mates and begin to build nests, the dawn chorus gradually diminishes until it comes to an end, usually somewhere towards the end of July. There's also a 'dusk chorus', a similar outbreak of birdsong at the close of the day, but it's not usually so noticeable.

Night singers

There are a handful of unusual species which sing at night. Most people are familiar with the idea of the nightingale as a night singer, although it's increasingly rare to hear one. Nightjars and corncrakes also sing nocturnally, and all three species are migratory; it's thought they sing to attract mates who are flying over homing territory at night. A few other species are quick to be prompted to sing by very low light levels. Robins, for example, are often heard at night and sometimes take up posts by streetlights or other artificial light sources. And although it's much simpler and has far fewer sounds, their song is often mistaken for a nightingale's.

Corncrake,
Crex crex

BEATING THE PLANES

Some recent studies have shown that songbirds are changing their habits to help them to adapt to urbanized surroundings. A study in the *Public Library of Science* journal in 2014 found that birds had been recorded singing at a higher pitch, apparently to make their songs more audible amongst the traffic noises in town, while another, published in *Behavioural Ecology* in the same year, conducted around the airports of Berlin, Barcelona, Madrid, Malaga and Valencia, discovered that birds living nearby were getting up almost half an hour earlier to sing before the major air traffic of the day started. Researchers worried that a longer and earlier song cycle might take its toll on the birds' energy and well-being, but also expressed optimism about their high levels of adaptability.

Should I feed the birds year-round?

IT MAKES SENSE that you should offer a well-stocked feeding station through the winter, when most birds' natural diet is thin on the ground, sometimes literally. But what about at other times of the year, when there seems to be an abundance of bugs, seeds and fruit around: do birds need the boost of your bird table then, too?

The year in food
If you look at birds' energy requirements season by season, it quickly becomes clear that supplementary food is welcome year-round. While the general scarcity of most foods makes it especially welcome in winter, life is demanding in spring, summer and autumn, too.

Spring into summer
In spring, the quick-fire sequence of mating, nesting and raising chicks makes heavy calls on the parent birds' resources, and in years where the weather is cold or wet, supplementary food can help to ensure that they raise healthy chicks. Just refrain from putting out peanuts, bread or fat during this time as these are harmful

Once you've started to feed the birds you shouldn't abruptly stop, whatever the season. If you do, they may waste energy calling at a 'reliable' food supply, only to find that they need to look elsewhere. And there are plenty of different reasons to offer food year-round.

if fed to young birds in the nest. When those chicks fledge, well-stocked feeders can be useful to set them on their way. Although there's usually plenty of food about in summer, there's also more competition for it, as fledglings turn into adults.

Summer into autumn
In late summer, the garden will become quieter, appearing as though the birds have left en masse. That's not the case: what's happening is that the fledglings are losing their 'baby' feathers to their adult plumage, and many adult birds are simply moulting,

House sparrow,
Passer domesticus

causing them to keep a lower profile. You may glimpse some familiar visitors looking bedraggled, but moulting is necessary to replace feathers that have become worn and damaged. It calls for a good deal of energy to grow new ones, so birds need to have easy access to food as they moult. Migrants have the quickest moults, as they have to leave for winter quarters before colder weather sets in; year-round residents may take five or six weeks to regrow their plumage. They will appreciate discreet feeding (food placed around the roots of border plants, or in quieter corners) during this vulnerable time.

As the moult completes and autumn turns into winter, garden birds once again need extra energy to survive the colder weather and the year comes full circle.

FAT: GOOD OR BAD FOR BIRDS?

Ever since bird tables became big business, with dozens of different offerings from sunflower seeds to fat balls on offer, it's been assumed that feeding fat, calorie-rich food in even very small quantities must benefit birds. Three research studies, two (in 2010 and 2013) that studied blue tits and great tits, and one (in 2013) studying the great spotted woodpecker, looked at whether birds benefited when fed supplementary fat and showed some mixed results: while the woodpecker bred more young with the additional fat in its diet, both the tit species were less productive with the extra fat. As yet, there hasn't been sufficient research to establish whether feeding birds fat is a bad idea but with further study, the picture may change.

Whatever ultimately emerges, there's one kind of fat that should never be offered: soft cooking fat (for example, the fatty pan juices left over from cooking a chicken or meat roast) is bad for birds. Its gluey texture can mean that they inadvertently smear it on their feathers while feeding and the residue can seriously damage the waterproofing that's essential to keep birds protected against the elements. Remember, if you do opt to offer fatty foods at your bird feeder, stick to the hard fats, such as suet balls, or a little grated hard cheese (robins seem to find the latter particularly irresistible).

All my garden robins have red breasts; are they all male?

MOST GARDENERS HAVE FOUND THEMSELVES with a robin for company when they're digging over a bed: it will perch nearby and swoop down to gobble up any worms or other insects the spade uncovers. And the robin invariably has a red breast; are the females less visible, or do they share the same plumage?

Why the red breast?

Robins are famously territorial and the red chest feathers are puffed out aggressively when they need to defend their space against robin competition. The stronger the show they can put on, the less likelihood that they will need to fight for their territory and, given that clashes can sometimes result in a fight to the death, the more effective the display the better.

Although robins pair and mate early in the year, once paired, they take on different roles: the male is in charge of territorial defence and the female builds the nest on her own. The pair share the raising of the chicks, often having multiple broods, but separate

You're probably seeing both male and female adult robins. Both have red breasts, and the shared plumage is just one of the ways in which they differ from most other garden birds. Only juvenile robins lack the distinctive red bib.

again in late summer. The females then become territorial in their own right, defending their own space for winter with just as much fanfare as the males. Oddest of all, having spent the day patrolling their solitary territory, robins have been observed roosting communally in close groups of up to 20 individuals, perhaps the very ones that have been their foes during the day.

◀ Social and bold in the UK, *Erithacus rubecula*'s habitat range goes from the fringes of Siberia across Europe and down to North Africa. Its European persona is different from its British one – in Europe it's known as an elusive woodland species which isn't very easily spotted.

Is natural food best for birds?

EVEN IF YOU OFFER the birds in your garden plenty of supplementary food, they're still likely to get most of their supplies from natural sources such as plants and trees. What should you plant to maximize what they can gather from your garden?

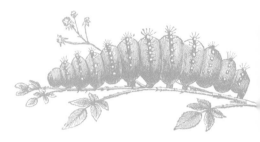

The trick when it comes to avian visitors is to make sure that there's something for everyone, whatever their preferred diet. Ideally, this means having shrubs and, if space permits, fruit trees (for berries, hips, haws and fruit), all of which are enjoyed by a variety of species, as well as plants that will offer plenty of seed heads (including teasels, thistles and perhaps some sunflowers for the seedeaters) and of course flowering plants and caterpillar food-plants for a good supply of insects and caterpillars – essential for raising successful broods and a favourite diet for insect-eating birds, including summer visitors such as flycatchers.

Give thrushes a stone at the back of the border and they are likely to use it to crack snails from their shells. Many birds are opportunistic feeders: robins and blackbirds, for example, will happily feast on worms, small beetles and other invertebrates on the ground, but will also take full seasonal advantage of fruit such as cherries, apples and pears, both on the tree (as some gardeners know to their cost) and as windfalls.

In winter, you may be surprised by exotic avian visitors, such as the waxwing, which arrives in crowds some years and not at all in others. Flocks may be spotted in surprisingly urban settings: supermarket car parks, for example, where the attraction is the municipal plantings of berry-rich shrubs such as pyracanthas.

If you look around your garden, you'll probably see opportunities for birds to find a tasty worm or snail and plenty of plants that benefit birds either directly (with seeds, fruit and berries) or indirectly, by attracting invertebrates that are a favoured food source. All you need to do is spot the gaps and fill them in.

Can I cater for caterpillars?

MANY BUTTERFLIES, and to an extent moths, will visit a wide range of flowering plants for the nectar they feed on as adults; most don't depend on just one or two varieties. But without eggs and caterpillars, there wouldn't be any adult Lepidoptera, and the food plants on which eggs are laid, and on which the caterpillars feed, often aren't those they will use as adults.

Caterpillar food plants

Before you start looking at how caterpillar-friendly your garden planting is, it's worth checking which species you can expect to find in your geographical area. For example, if you live quite far north, your garden is less likely to attract peacock butterflies or holly blues than one sited further south, even if you make sure you have a good supply of nettles for the first and ivy for the second. Red admirals, on the other hand, are found across a very wide geographical area, so are one of the species most likely to breed in your garden if you offer the right plants.

Egg spotting

Lepidoptera eggs are tiny and can be hard to see unless you know what you're looking for. They're usually laid on the host plant's leaves (mostly on the underside of the leaf, although sometimes on top) or stems, or in the case of shrubs and trees, in the cracks of bark. They can be as small as pinheads, oval or round shaped, sometimes with ridges and come in a whole spectrum of colours, from

In order to have adult butterflies and moths, there need to be caterpillars. Unlike that of the parents, the caterpillar diet consists of leaves only, and often quite specific leaves. Encourage the caterpillar part of the life cycle by supplying the plants that butterflies and moths will lay their eggs on, and that will subsequently feed their larvae.

creamy white to pale green, bright yellow or orange, and may be laid, depending on the species, at any time between May and August. They take between one and three weeks to hatch, again depending on the species and the weather. Spot them by examining leaves gently on both sides. Once found, try not to disturb the plant while you're waiting for the caterpillars to hatch.

WHO LIKES WHAT?

Many native wildflowers are known to be used for breeding butterflies and moths. It makes sense to grow plenty of these. Some can be introduced as small plug plants into an existing wildflower or meadow area. If you're lucky enough to have a hazel or hawthorn hedge bordering your garden, it's likely to be popular with a number of moth species. Goat willow trees (*Salix caprea*), also known as pussy willow, are also very attractive to moths.

Some other popular food plants for caterpillars include:

▲ The orange tip butterfly (*Anthocharis cardamines*) on lady's smock.

• **Lady's smock (*Cardamine pratensis*)**, also known as cuckoo flower. Preferred by orange tip and green-veined white butterflies.

• **Common nettle (*Urtica dioica*)** A favourite, eaten by the caterpillars of peacock (below right), red admiral, comma and small tortoiseshell butterflies, and burnished brass, cream-spot tiger and scarlet tiger moths. Check out what grows in your garden's vicinity – you probably won't want to let nettles stage a takeover in your garden, but if you're near a brownfield site with large nettle patches, there's a strong chance that you already have a breeding site nearby.

• **Bird's foot trefoil (*Lotus corniculatus*)** Common blue caterpillars will feed on this, as will those of the six-spot burnet moth.

• **Lady's bedstraw (*Galium verum*)** Appealing in its own right for its frothy and strong-scented yellow flowers, this also offers a habitat for an enormous range of caterpillars, particularly those of moth species, including the showy hummingbird hawk, the small elephant hawk and the elegantly marked silver Y.

What's the point of a moth trap?

BUTTERFLIES AREN'T HARD TO OBSERVE; you can follow them round the garden, wait for them to rest on a flower or leaf, have a quick look, then wait till they next settle. It's more difficult to moth-watch, or at least it is in the case of the nocturnal species, which are hugely in the majority. How can you create an opportunity to look at them in detail?

Commercially produced moth traps vary in price. At the high end they can be expensive and are mainly used by professionals, but there are some simple and affordable models.

How moth traps work
They all operate on the same principle: moths are attracted by a very bright light and, as they fly towards it, are funnelled through a one-way entrance into a dark box or tub which contains cardboard egg boxes for them to rest on, where they can safely be contained until you open it in the morning. The moths are then released unharmed, either in a dark corner to give them

Professional lepidopterists (and many amateur enthusiasts) use a light trap. It catches night-flying insects, including moths, without hurting them, allowing you a close-up look before releasing them and will let you discover which species are using your garden.

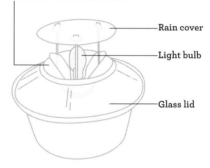

The moth approaches the light and then slides down into the tub

Rain cover

Light bulb

Glass lid

cover or later, at dusk (to avoid predators swooping in) the following evening. The bulbs used often give off actinic light, which isn't strongly visible to the human eye; in traps where non-actinic bulbs are used, the degree of light is very bright and harsh, which may be an annoyance when your garden is overlooked.

If you look them up, you'll see three types of moth trap: the most expensive, the Robinson trap, is a light mounted over a funnel fixed above a rigid plastic tub; next down, in both price and efficiency, the Skinner trap is a wooden box shape, with a similar bulb but more sloped

Scalloped oak moth,
Crocallis elinguaria

sides; while the third and cheapest type, the Heath trap, has a tube bulb mounted vertically over a rectangular box, usually made of metal.

Starting out

You can improvise a rudimentary moth-viewing station by hanging a white sheet over a washing line and shining a very bright torch at it. A variety of nocturnal insects will be disorientated by the light and land on the sheet. With its excuse-to-stay-up-late possibilities, it's a good way to introduce children to the insects that are active at night, although it's unlikely that any will stay still enough for serious identification. A cloudy night with little or no moonlight and not much wind offers the best conditions for moth spotting.

If you graduate to a trap, read up on the different types: start at the economical end, then upgrade if moth-watching becomes a serious hobby. Check out your local wildlife organizations, too – some will loan a moth trap to give you a taster. A moth identification guide will help you put names to the larger moths, wonderful sounding ones such as feathered thorn, scalloped oak and white ermine.

FIVE MOTH TRAP BASICS

• Keep your electrics dry. The electrical connections in any moth trap should be waterproof and safe. Ideally you should run an extension from your mains electricity supply; you can use a battery, but it's crucial to keep everything dry. Moth trapping, in any case, isn't recommended in heavy rain.

• Set your trap up in as dark a spot as possible, so you won't have lots of competing light sources.

• Spread a white sheet on the ground to put the trap on. This ensures that insects that settle around the trap won't be trodden on when you go to check it.

• Check the trap as early in the morning as possible. Moths can be emptied into observation containers to allow you to have a proper look at them.

• When you've looked at it, let the 'catch' go; don't keep moths for longer than necessary: they need to feed and breed.

Is pollen as important as nectar?

POLLINATORS NEED NECTAR to nourish them in their journey from one flower to another, but many are also collecting pollen for their young to eat and, on occasion, to eat themselves. Which is the more important substance for wildlife?

Nectar-feeding butterflies and moths pollinate by accident; they don't eat or collect pollen. Bees, on the other hand, mostly drink nectar while out and about and collect pollen for stores for both larvae and adult bees back at home. Their collection methods vary, from gathering it in pollen baskets to (in the case of some of the smaller species) eating it, then regurgitating it up to stock up their larval cells once back at their nests. Other insects eat pollen, too, including some species of hoverflies and the tiny, metallic pollen beetles which are sometimes found in large numbers on flowers such as sweet peas.

Nectar is the sugary, quick-fix food for instant energy, whereas pollen is packed with protein, along with a range of other useful ingredients such as amino acids. Each plays a crucial part within the insect food web, but they have different roles.

Which flowers supply the best food?

There is still plenty of research to be done on pollen, but studies have shown that its protein content can vary widely, from under 10 per cent to around 45 per cent of each sticky grain. The higher the protein content, the more nutritious the pollen, and other research has established that bumblebees recognize and prefer those flowers which carry the highest quality. Top-quality pollen tends to come from plants in the huge Papilionaceae family, which includes peas, beans and all varieties of clover.

From the gardener's point of view, advice for planting for pollinators remains the same: plant as wide a

Wild rose/
dog rose,
Rosa canina

variety of flowers as possible, with a mixture of flower shapes, ranging from the simple, easy-access bowl shape of, say, a wild rose or a buttercup, which appeals to a wide range of insects, to those that call for specialists, such as the tubular flowers of foxgloves or lipped flowers of broom, which are especially suited to long-tongued bumblebees. Whether or not plants are native – that is, indigenous – doesn't seem to matter to pollinators, provided that they offer accessible food, suited to their various feeding habits.

Common foxglove,
Digitalis purpurea

WHY IS POLLEN ALWAYS YELLOW?

It isn't. While the majority of pollen is yellow, it also comes in blue, orange and white in a few plants. It's true, though, that the vast majority is yellow. In the past it was thought that the sole reason for this was because it appealed most strongly to pollinators (who can't see colours on the red spectrum). Wind-pollinated plants mostly have yellow pollen, too, so it seemed unlikely that this was the only reason. The yellow in the substance that covers pollen grains comes from chemicals called flavonoids and these protect the grain from UV-B rays, like a kind of sunscreen. If pollen deteriorates before it does its job, it's more likely to go on to form a part of a seed which will have undesirable mutations. The yellow of pollen may therefore prove to be a side effect of its protective coating, rather than something that has evolved purely to attract pollinators.

Why should I love my weeds?

MOST OF US HAVE HEARD the truism that a weed is simply a plant growing in the wrong place, and you'll also have been told that many 'weeds' are in fact highly beneficial to wildlife. Should you love weeds indiscriminately, or are there some that deserve a timely heave-ho?

The good, the bad and the ugly

You probably already know that dandelions are worth making room for, to a point at least. They pay their way by flowering indefatigably across a very long season, thus offering a rich source of pollen when there isn't much else around. And they represent the good end of weed life: although they self-seed freely, they're easily pulled up and they aren't so vigorous as to suppress other species. Other 'weeds' whose wildlife value outweighs the

Spear thistle,
Cirsium vulgare

For the wildlife gardener, biodiversity is always the most important rule. The more varied the habitats and plant species you can introduce to your garden the better. And many so-called weeds have a part to play in that. Some, though, are invasive to the point that your garden's biodiversity is actually reduced and in a managed habitat such as a garden, weeding them out is sensible.

relatively minor inconvenience of keeping them under control are ragwort (*Senecio jacobaea*) (which isn't desirable in cut pasture, as it is poisonous to grazing animals, but which can be a valuable wildlife asset in the garden), cat's-ear (*Hypochaeris radicata*) and spear thistle (*Cirsium vulgare*).

No one will suggest that you love the weeds at the 'bad' end of the scale. In fact, in some cases, it's an offence to allow them to escape from your garden.

This applies, for example, to Japanese knotweed (*Fallopia japonica*), which was originally imported as a decorative garden novelty but which, with unstoppably vigorous growth and no natural predators, has become a huge problem all over the UK and Europe. Perhaps less notorious but equally hard to get rid of is horsetail (*Equisetum arvense*). It's the bane of allotment keepers and gardeners, spreading by rhizomes that can run as deep as 2m (6$\frac{1}{2}$ft) under the soil. While you can weaken horsetail with repeated, regular hoeing, the depth of its roots make it almost impossible to dig out and many gardeners settle for keeping it down rather than trying to eradicate it altogether. Both of these are examples of weeds that actively limit or choke other species; they're simply too successful to work in a mixed habitat.

SOLVING THE HIMALAYAN BALSAM PROBLEM

Like Japanese knotweed, Himalayan balsam (*Impatiens glandulifera*) was originally introduced to British and European gardens in the mid-19th century as an ornamental plant. Bees love its attractive pink flowers, but since it has escaped from the garden setting and established itself in open countryside, it's become a problem. It is one of the fastest-growing annuals, whose speed of growth and size – up to 3m (10ft) tall – means it grabs light and nutrients from less thuggish plants and spreads its seeds by means of exploding pods, each of which flings its contents a distance of anything up to 6m (20ft). The good news is that, unlike species that spread by means of rhizomes, it has shallow roots and is easily pulled up; but the seeds are viable for several years and spread readily along streams and other water courses. There are some plans to eradicate it by means of biological controls – a rust to which it's susceptible – but the speed and range of its spread demonstrates what can happen when plants go rogue.

My garden's all wall; will wildlife use it?

QUITE A FEW TOWN GARDENS, squashed in at the planning stage, consist of a small area surrounded by walls. Or maybe you live in a flat or apartment with only opportunity for planting on a balcony or up a wall. If that describes your plot, what can you do to ensure that it's as beneficial to wildlife – from birds to bugs – as possible?

Firethorn, *Pyracantha*

Climbing plants can offer food and shelter to numerous species, from minute invertebrates to nesting birds, and vertical walls aren't any deterrent to winged wildlife. Avoid the arid so-called rain shadow or 'drought zone' directly at the base of the wall by planting them 30–45cm (12–18in) out, propping them inwards if necessary until they start to climb. If you have no access to soil, choose a generous container for your climbers, at least 30cm (12in) in diameter. Some climbers will scramble naturally, but others will need support such as wires, trellis or some netting to guide them upwards.

What about shrubs?

Pyracanthas (*Pyracantha* [Saphyr Orange] 'Cadange') is perhaps not so much technically a climber as an upright evergreen shrub. They are easy to train upwards by tying the flexible younger (and less spiky) shoots onto wires. They offer very dense, spiny shelter along with lavish quantities of white flowers in spring, which are followed by long-lasting bright red, orange or yellow berries. Those with berries in the brightest red/orange colour range seem to find most favour with birds, and this is a particularly vivid variety.

Even a plain brick wall or a high fence can have some attractions for wildlife; if it gets sun at some point during the day, it can be a good basking spot for insects, for example. Grow some climbers up it, though, and you'll quadruple its appeal.

TOP CLIMBERS FOR WILDLIFE

Honeysuckle (*Lonicera periclymenum*) This is a
vigorous climber with richly scented flowers (right) for
pollinators plus plenty of bright red berries in autumn
for the birds and dense, rambling growth, offering
shelter for both roosting and nesting. And a side benefit is
that the bark at the base of the plant peels off in shreds and
is sometimes used as nest lining.

Clematis (*Clematis cirrhosa* 'Freckles'). This winter-flowering clematis
has delicate cream flowers speckled with deep pink. The flowers are
long-lasting, often opening in November and lasting until February. They're
useful as gap-fillers for pollinators, such as solitary bees and bumblebee
queens, who are emerging hungrily from hibernation and finding little in
flower. And the foliage is evergreen, so it offers year-round shelter.

Ivy (*Hedera helix*). Although it may not sound the most exciting choice,
ivy has a huge amount to offer all kinds of wildlife, including the dense
cover it provides for a range of species, from nesting birds to hibernating
butterflies; the pollen-rich flowers, valuable for being one of the last
flowers of the season; and the berries that come late enough to fill the
hungry gap towards the end of winter. There's the added bonus that it's
not hard to grow and will thrive in less-than-ideal shady conditions. Ivy's
reputation for damaging walls is largely undeserved, too: unless a wall is
already crumbling, it's unlikely to do it any damage. And smaller forms
of ivy are available if you do not have a large wall to cover.

Jasmine (*Jasminum officinale*). An enthusiastic climber (left) covered in
white flowers that exude a very sweet scent, summer jasmine has a
strong appeal for pollinators. It needs shelter and a
sunny wall (it isn't tough enough to withstand a hard
frost), but if you can provide these, it will
flourish in open soil or in a container and
will grow to a height of up to 5m (16ft).

Do green roofs work?

GREEN ROOFS IN DOMESTIC GARDENS, particularly on garden sheds and offices, have had a lot of positive press over the last few years. Are they effective in adding an extra wildlife dimension to the garden?

Green roofs attract a whole range of invertebrates and are often popular with the birds who feed on them, too. They also make use of rainwater, rather than allowing it simply to wash off and add to the raised groundwater levels that have contributed to many flooding problems over the last 20 years. And while larger green roofs are best left to the experts, it's possible to construct a green roof on a modest scale yourself, to go on a small shed or even to top off a bin storage area.

When you make a green roof, you are creating a new growing space where there wasn't one before and which will add to the biodiversity in your garden. The shallow, lightweight nature of a green roof also means that it supplies a growing environment that's quite low in nutrients – perfect for plants for which cultivated garden soil is often too rich.

Structure and planting

It's important to check that the shed or other structure is strong enough to take the additional weight (even if you're planning to make the roof yourself, the weight-bearing aspect should be checked by a professional).

The simplest form for a flat green roof consists of a wooden frame made to fit tightly around the edge of the supporting roof surface, and to sit 3–5cm (1–2in) proud of the existing level. This is slotted over a double layer, the first of thick plastic (pond liner works well), the second of root-proof membrane. Once on the roof, the frame is filled with substrate, a lightweight planting medium, then either covered with a layer of sedums (the drought-resistant forms that are most commonly used on green roofs) or planted up with suitable wildflower mix or plug plants.

A green roof made up of mixed sedums can have an attractive patchwork effect.

How can I ID insect larvae?

GRUBS, CATERPILLARS, WORMS that seem to have legs...
It can be hard identifying insects in their adult form, but when
it comes to their immature, larval state, it can seem near-
impossible. How can you narrow the categories down to get
at least an idea of what you're looking at?

Here's where to start.
Eruciform: Eruciform larvae
are caterpillar-shaped, with a defined
head at one end and two sorts of legs:
three pairs of usually short, spiky 'true'
legs at the front end and five pairs of
'pro legs', that look like mobile stumps,
further down the body.

Elateriform: A hard-bodied
worm-like structure but with legs.
Elateriform larvae usually belong to
one or other member of the (huge)
beetle family.

Scarabeiform: Fat-bodied, curved
larvae with legs on the thorax only
and a defined head. Again, most
scarabeiform larvae are beetles.

Vermiform: Grub-like and legless,
some vermiform larvae have a defined
head, while others don't. They belong
to a wide range of invertebrates,
including beetles (especially weevils),
bees, ants, moths, true flies and
grasshoppers.

The fifth form is Campodeiform.
While the other four categories are
all at least slightly grub- or wormlike,
campodeiform larvae resemble tiny
dragons. They're fast movers, with
efficient legs, flat, segmented bodies

There are fewer larval forms
than you might think: basically,
insect larvae divide into five
main body forms. However,
to pin down a specific larva
beyond its broad grouping,
you may have to invest in a
field guide.

Eruciform

Vermiform

Elateriform

Scarabeiform

Campodeiform

and visible antennae. The larvae
of both lacewings and ladybirds are
campodeiform: look for the nearest
aphid group and you'll see these tiny,
active creatures in amongst them,
gobbling them up.

Where do bumblebees live?

BUMBLEBEES, LIKE HONEYBEES, are social bees who live in colonies, although the latter are much smaller than those of honeybees, with numbers in the low hundreds at most, compared to the 50,000-plus bees in a healthy honeybee colony. We're used to seeing a range of bumblebee species foraging among the flowers in the garden, but where do they actually live?

Looking for a site

Queens of the earliest bumblebee species will start the search for a nest in early spring, and they're often spotted flying low over the ground on reconnaissance missions. Gardens with a good supply of nectar-rich flowers will be popular sites, although the nests are often very discreet and not easy to spot. They're sometimes located under sheds or in burrows at the corners of buildings or alongside drainpipes. Bumblebees aren't aggressive unless they feel directly threatened so if you find a nest, don't disturb it, and mark the site to ensure that nobody else does. They're maintained for around three

Bumblebees live in nests, found and chosen by the queen early in the year. Many species opt for pre-existing holes or burrows, often below ground; abandoned mouse nests are popular.

months, after which time most of the inhabitants will die. Any new young queens that have been raised will mate, then depart to find somewhere for solo hibernation, from which they will emerge in the spring to start the whole cycle over again.

◄ The cells in bumblebee nests don't have the same neat hexagonal look as those of honeybees, but the nest structure is broadly similar.

Unexpected tenants

There's one particular bumblebee, found all over Europe and a recent, though widespread, arrival in UK gardens, which will sometimes take up residence in a nest box put up for birds. It's the tree bumblebee (*Bombus hypnorum*) and it has easily recognized markings: a white tail, a black abdomen and a solid ginger-orange thorax. Its natural nesting site would be in a tree hollow or crevice, high above the ground (unlike most bumblebee species who like to nest on or under the ground). It seems particularly keen on boxes that have an old bird's nest that it can use as a base, and it can be quite determined when setting up home; there are even some accounts of bees evicting pairs of blue tits and staging a nest takeover. You'll know the bees are there when, rather than parent birds, you notice a small group buzzing or 'dancing' around the entrance to the box (these are the stingless males competing for the attentions of the queen, so there's no danger of being stung). It's best to leave them undisturbed until the nest empties naturally in late July or early August.

MASTERS OF SCENT

Both bumbles and honeybees have a very refined sense of smell. And minute quantities of a sticky secretion from their feet enable them to leave a personalized trail – known as a scent mark – on the surfaces they touch. The results of a series of experiments carried out at the University of Bristol (published in 2017) established that bumblebees could identify the scent of their own footprints, those of other bees from their own colony and those of unknown bees. Scientists believe that this ability helps them distinguish between those flowers which have been recently visited (and emptied of nectar) and those which haven't recently had much insect traffic and are therefore likely to be rewarding to visit.

▼ The tree bumblebee (*Bombus hypnorum*) sometimes nests in a bird box – once in residence, they're easily spotted flying around the entrance.

Chapter 2

On (and in) the Ground

What's the best boost for earthworks?

AS ALL GARDENERS KNOW, worms are good for the soil, and a healthy worm population is an excellent signifier that all is well below the surface. But if you haven't spotted many worms, does it mean there's a problem? And how many different kinds of worms should there be in a garden anyway?

Earthworms are more varied than you might think – there are 27 species found in the UK alone. All earthworms appreciate a habitat with plenty of organic material, so regular applications of compost and leaf mould will help them to continue conditioning the soil. Damp, clay-based soils naturally support more worms than dry sandy ones, but even the latter can be enriched with additional compost and leaf mould.

Wormholes

There are three types of soil-living earthworm, each with a different lifestyle. On the surface you'll find epigeic worms which hide out in layers of dead leaves or other vegetation. Both endogeic and anecic species live under the surface. Endogeic worms make their way horizontally through the earth, creating tunnels, while anecic species form vertical burrows and may be found up to 3m (10ft) below the soil's surface. They come to the surface at night in search of dead leaves. If you see a leaf that appears

to have been pulled halfway into the soil, it is usually the work of an anecic worm gathering its next meal.

There's a fourth group: compost worms, most often seen hanging out in your compost heap. They don't live in the soil, but seek out warm, damp environments where they can consume decomposing vegetable matter. Soil-living earthworms tend to be pale in colour, whereas composting worms, such as brandling or tiger worms, tend to be bright red and stripy.

Worm activities are very simple: they burrow, eat and excrete. But their excretions contain concentrated quantities of nutrients and bacteria;

Two words: organic matter. That's what it takes to keep earthworms healthy and working hard to keep your soil in good order. But not all earthworms are equal, and different types have quite separate lifestyles.

up to five times more than is found in the earth around them. In burrowing through the soil they also introduce oxygen and improve drainage, enriching and conditioning as they go. Ecologists view worms as an indicator of soil health: when a site is rich in worms, it's fertile, with a diverse population of microorganisms.

Worms also play an important part in the garden food web, appearing on the preferred menus of a whole range of other species, from thrushes to hedgehogs.

A 'WHO'S WHO' OF GARDEN EARTHWORMS

You may never have looked closely at your garden worm population, but if you do, you will find the species are quite distinct. Here are six you may spot, plus some pointers on how to identify them. If you see a worm that doesn't have the characteristic mid-body fleshy area, or saddle, it's an immature specimen and isn't ready for identification yet.

Epigeic:
Red-headed worm (*Lumbricus rubellus*) Reddish brown from the saddle to the tip of the head, with a grey tail end. Lives in piles of dead leaves and on the soil surface.
Up to 6.5cm (3in) when still.

Endogeic:
Grey worm (*Aporrectodea caliginosa*) Recognized by the three broad stripes in different shades of grey along its body.
Up to 6cm (2.5in) long when still.

Green worm (*Allolobophora chlorotica*) Colour ranges from pale grey-green to grey. Up to 5cm (2in) long when still.

Rosy-tipped worm (*Aporrectodea rosea*) Pale at one end, with an orange saddle area and, as the name implies, a greyish-pink head end. Up to 6cm (2.5in) long when still.

Anecic:
Lob worm (*Lumbricus terrestris*), also known as the 'nightcrawler' (below), or common earthworm. Sometimes over 12cm (5in) long, the lob worm is the largest UK native.

Black-headed worm (*Aporrectodea longa*) A long, thin worm, very dark in colour, though lightening from the purplish-black head down to a dark grey 'tail' end. Up to 12cm (5in) long when still.

How can I help hedgehogs?

THE EUROPEAN HEDGEHOG (*Erinaceous europaeus*) has been a popular garden visitor for centuries. And the loss of much of its natural wild habitat – hedges, copses, fields and woodland – means that domestic gardens have become valuable refuges. As a gardener, what can you do to help the hedgehog?

The gardener's friend

Across Europe, hedgehog populations are struggling; in the UK alone numbers have fallen by over half in the last two decades. There is some evidence that urban hedgehogs are doing better than their rural counterparts, and gardeners can help this trend. Hedgehogs repay their host by keeping caterpillars in check and eating slugs and snails.

Safety first

Cut out chemicals wherever possible: use organic or biological pest controls and water-based, environmentally-friendly preservatives on any fences or other wood surfaces hedgehogs may come in contact with. Don't leave hazards such as loose netting or wire lying about: hedgehogs get tangled and as their natural response to danger is to curl up, they're not good at freeing themselves. Make sure that any water, such as a pond or water feature, has got easy access out as well as in (hedgehogs are good swimmers, but they need a slope or support to climb out).

Hedgehog hideaways

After safety, shelter and food are top of the list. Hedgehogs like piles of leaves, compost heaps and untended spots where they'll find both food and shelter. So leave a few corners of the garden untouched. For hibernation and raising young, the crawl spaces under garden sheds and decking are popular, so check carefully before undertaking any renovation work to outdoor buildings. Compost heaps are favoured spots for hibernating hedgehogs, so do any compost turning slowly and carefully. Hedgehogs don't reliably make use of artificial boxes but it may be worth trying one out in a new garden where natural shelter is lacking. Construct a shelter of wood or

AEasy access is a good starting point: make sure hedgehogs can move in and out of your garden. And create a welcoming, safe, chemical-free environment, with some undisturbed corners that will offer both shelter and feeding opportunities.

securely propped bricks, with a short tunnel entrance and solid walls and roof. You can offer a starter bedding of hay, although most hedgehogs will prefer to import their own materials.

To feed hedgehogs, either opt for specialized food or meaty cat or dog food, served alongside a dish of fresh water. Milk is a definite no-no (it gives hedgehogs diarrhoea), and although dried fruit is a treat, it's really too sugary. Mealworms should only be given sparingly. Setting up a feeding station will give you best chance of spotting hedgehogs. Cats will usually sniff a hedgehog and then leave it alone, whereas dogs will occasionally attack them. If you're lucky enough to establish regular visits, it's a good idea to keep your dogs, and if possible cats, inside at night.

Hedgehogs thrive on a lack of interference. If you've offered security, food and shelter, chances are good that you'll get hedgehog visitors. Be prepared to sit in the dark for a while: healthy hedgehogs are strictly nocturnal and only emerge at dusk.

MAKE A HEDGEHOG GATEWAY

With the threat to their wilder habitat, gardens have become increasingly important for hedgehogs. But they roam quite widely for their size – a healthy hedgehog will cover around 3km (2 miles) or even more in a night – so they need easy access in and out of your garden. Get together with neighbours and organize a 'hog highway', with hedgehog holes through a chain of gardens.

How to do it
A hedgehog gateway is simply a hole cut into the bottom of a fence where it's easy to pass from one garden to another. It should be around 13cm (5in) high and at least as wide, preferably located in a sheltered corner of the garden. Cut a new hole in the fencing panel with a coping saw and sand off any very rough edges.

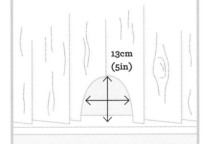

13cm
(5in)

Q Should I leave snails alone?

SNAILS GENERALLY DON'T get quite such bad press as slugs, but their hungry habits may still be an annoyance, especially when their attentions are directed towards favourite plants. So what's the best way to manage your relationship with snails (not to mention the snails themselves)?

A The best route is to encourage more predators, from toads to thrushes, into your garden; snails are a valued food source for many animals. Most traditional anti-snail remedies aren't effective.

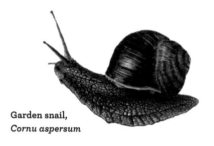

Garden snail,
Cornu aspersum

If you're tempted to try some of the well-known home hacks to dissuade your garden snails, don't underestimate the highly protective nature of the thick slime that helps gastropods glide along. The results of a study carried out by the RHS into a range of snail and slug deterrents were published in 2018 and found that a whole range of popular 'fixes' had little or no effect. Lettuces protected using a variety of measures including copper tape, wool pellets, crushed eggshells, pine bark mulch and horticultural grit ended up with exactly the same level of snail and slug damage as those left unprotected: none of the rough, sharp or (in the case of copper) shocking sensations under the snails' muscular 'feet' seemed to discourage them. Interestingly, the lettuces surrounded by wool pellets and pine bark mulch grew 50 per cent bigger than the others, benefitting from the additional mulch and fertilizer.

Both toads and frogs will tackle snails provided they are small enough to swallow whole. The shells are crushed into fragments and passed in their droppings.

Snail measures that work

The RHS study concluded that the best way to combat snails was to encourage their natural predators into the garden. Hedgehogs and toads will eat snails as part of their diet. Thrushes also love snails, and they'll sharply tap their prey on stones to crack the shells and get at their meal. If you don't already have stone surfaces in your garden, introduce one or two flat 'anvil' stones for thrushes to make use of.

The nematodes that can work well in bringing down the numbers of slugs in the garden have a limited effectiveness on snails, because snails live on the soil's surface rather than under it, where the nematodes operate. Some species of beetles and beetle larvae eat snails (*Cychrus caraboides* is even named 'snail hunter') and beetle-friendly habitats will encourage a healthy population. They include that of the increasingly rare European glow worm (*Lampyris noctiluca*), whose tiny green lights you may occasionally see on a dark summer's evening, blinking in vegetation along a path's edge and which, despite its name, is actually a beetle. Larvae dispatch their victims by injecting

HOW MANY?

Around 100 different species of snail are found in the UK, and hundreds more across Europe. They range in size from minute specimens the size of a pinhead to the grey-brown common garden snail, seen everywhere and responsible for the lion's share of plant damage caused by snails (don't forget that slugs also eat their fair share). Snail-spotting around the garden, you may be surprised at how many different types you see (during the day, look round empty pots and behind any ivy or other climbers), and you'll notice that some of the shells, especially those of the stripy banded snail species, are exceptionally pretty.

them with a paralysing substance, then suck out the contents of the shells.

Of course, you can also pick snails up and dispose of them yourself. Some gardeners drown them in a bucket of water; others, more kindly, rehome them in the compost heap (although they can't be guaranteed to stay there!). Snails are thought to lose their bearings about 20m (65ft) from any spot they're been moved from, so they may not return to the same place.

Ground beetle, *Cychrus caraboides*

Adult   **Larvae**

Who's living in my compost heap?

Compost heaps tend to be warm, humid and, for most of your garden fauna, full of things to eat. So it's not surprising that they're magnets for a huge number of animal species, from single-cell organisms to insects, amphibians, reptiles and even mammals.

You might argue that you can see slugs and snails in plenty of other sites in your garden, but there aren't many where their munching activities are welcomed, rather than deplored!

It's one of the most popular habitats in the garden for all kinds of animal life. Various species of slugs, snails, worms, woodlice and beetles set up house there, reptiles may both hibernate and breed in it, and it may also get other callers, from hedgehogs to weasels.

And if a lot of the other life in the compost heap is microscopic, there are also unusual visitors that you may not spot elsewhere.

Hot bed

The warmth may attract grass snakes or slow worms to feed, hibernate and even breed. If you want to be sure that you're identifying grass snakes (*Natrix* sp.) correctly, they're a yellowish-green colour and have two stripes – one yellow, one dark – around their necks (unlike adders, which have a highly

Slow worm,
Anguis fragilis

HIGH JUMPERS

Some of the most numerous creatures in your compost heap may be a group you've barely heard of: springtails (Collembola family). They're tiny, from under a millimetre to around 6mm (¼in) long, and are quick to take advantage of any damp habitat. If you disturb the compost surface, the springtails will be the ones that leap into the air, rather than scuttling to hide.

Springtails belong to a particular group: they're hexapods. They have six legs on the thorax but are also wingless, with internal mouths. Springtails have two body types: globular, which are near spherical, and linear, which have a longer, flatter shape. And they have some other unique features. First, these minute creatures can jump extraordinarily high, spring-boarded by a tail-like structure called a furcul. This is held close underneath the body by either hooks or a 'catch', depending on the species; when startled, the furcula is released, snaps back and somersaults the springtail high in the air. Second, they have special tube-like organs which, among other functions, probably help it to maintain its moisture levels.

Springtails in your compost heap are mostly detritivores, feeding on decomposing matter and helping to speed the decomposition process along. And they're also popular in the diets of others: beetles, snails and slugs, to name just a few.

characteristic pattern of dark 'V's running down their backs). Grass snakes are harmless to humans and if disturbed they may huff and puff or, more characteristically, play dead. They sometimes lay their eggs in the compost, which acts as an incubator, in early to mid-summer. These are easily spotted: greyish-white, spherical – around 2.5cm (1in) in diameter – and with a rough, suede-like texture. If you find some, cover them back up and don't disturb the compost for at least two months to give them a chance to hatch. Slow worms (*Anguis fragilis*) which, despite the name, are actually legless lizards, are shorter and more rounded in shape than snakes, and have very small scales, giving them a smooth, metallic appearance in beautiful shades of bronze and pewter. They give birth to live young inside a cocoon, and you may occasionally find the dried-out remnants of the latter, looking like empty papery packets.

Can I make a wildlife feature of my stony soil?

SOME GARDEN SOIL IS NATURALLY STONY, and many urban and suburban gardens were created by placing a layer of soil over building debris, meaning that rocks, bits of broken brick and so on keep turning up when you're digging or planting. Can you turn them to the advantage of your garden wildlife?

Larger stones – solo if really big, grouped if smaller – offer two advantages for wildlife: a basking surface on the upper, sun-facing side and a cool shelter underneath. Both aspects will appeal to plenty of different species.

How you use your stones depends on their size: medium-sized or large rocks can be piled up into a rough but stable 'cairn', leaving plenty of crevices and gaps for small creatures to go in and out. Even a mixture of rubble and old bricks can be put to use in this way, using the best-looking bits around the outside. A rock pile can emulate the conditions of a drystone wall (popular as a nesting site with small mammals such as mice, voles and shrews); if it's sited near a pond, it may attract frogs and newts, too. Sun-warmed stones will appeal to butterflies who enjoy a site they can bask in.

Smooth newt,
Lissotriton vulgaris

STONY, NOT ROCKY

What if the problem isn't large stones, but soil that is full of small ones? Thin, stony soil is likely to be free-draining, so turn it to your advantage. Plant drought-tolerant plants, which are often excellent for pollinators.

Is strimming safe?

STRIMMING IS AN EFFECTIVE WAY of managing longer grass and overgrown corners in the garden. It's sometimes used to create paths through garden 'meadows'. But does it pose a danger to your garden wildlife, and if so, are there ways to make it safer?

To ensure your garden wildlife isn't harmed by strimming or mowing, you need to go through a checking and safety drill before starting, then complete the job before the creatures that have left the area return.

Strimmers or mowers can cause a lot of damage if they're not used carefully: in an unlucky encounter, frogs, toads, hedgehogs and other small creatures don't tend to come out unscathed. Go through the following steps before you strim to make it as safe as you can:

Jumpers or fliers, like this shield bug, can easily escape from the strimmer, but it's best to plan to give slower movers time to escape as you work.

1 Choose a bright, sunny day. Although it may encourage reptiles to bask in the sun, they'll be more likely to slither away at speed when you start work, because their metabolisms are warmed up.

2 Walk the area you're going to cut shortly before you start. Walk from one corner of the patch to the other with a stick, sweeping it gently through the grass or foliage ahead of you.

3 For larger areas, strim from the centre outwards rather than trapping creatures in an ever-decreasing area of untrimmed vegetation.

4 Cut in two stages. In taller areas, take off half the growth first, then collect the debris and check again before strimming to the desired height. Don't cut too short; aim to leave at least 10cm (4in) of growth.

5 Leave a generous border. At least 30cm (12in) should be left around logs, rock piles or other garden features to act as a refuge for departing wildlife.

Should I love leaf litter?

WILDLIFE LOVES LEAF LITTER; it offers food or shelter for lots of different species, from worms to toads and voles. And most gardeners love leaf mould: it makes wonderful mulch and is a great soil enricher. But what's the best thing to do if you have a really huge quantity of fallen leaves? Should you leave them be, collect them up, redistribute them, have a bonfire, or take them off site altogether?

The leaves don't have to stay where they fall to do their work. If there's a thick layer of fallen leaves on a grassy wildflower bank, for instance, you might need to move them to avoid the flowers and grass rotting under their weight – but relocated to a hedge base or a woodland border, they'll be appreciated by plenty of small rodents and invertebrates.

If it's necessary, redistribute leaves to where the wildlife will appreciate them most – quieter garden corners, or piled at the bases of hedges or walls – or gather them to rot down gradually, then return them to the soil to be enjoyed by the worms and other life underground.

Piles of dead leaves benefit all kinds of animal life; voles excavate their shallow burrows under a good cover of leaf litter.

They can be shredded, too, and added to the compost heap or piled up to rot down gradually. Make an open container for them if you have the space – it will be appreciated by wildlife, too – or use sacks if you don't.

If you exhaust all the spots where you can redistribute leaf litter on your own plot, don't burn it: it sends all those nutrients up in smoke, while adding to air pollution. Share the goodness with someone else's garden instead, either directly, with a neighbour, or by sending them for green waste composting.

Tough leaves

Evergreen leaves take longer to rot down than deciduous ones, so if you have a lot of holly clippings, for example, and you don't have a shredder, you may want to make a separate heap for them.

Conifer needles, too, will rot down eventually; if you have enough

to collect, it's worth putting them in a separate pile – the eventual result will be a lime-free compost that will make the perfect mulch if you grow blueberries.

Needles, like the clippings from this yew, take a long time to rot down; if you have a lot of them, heap them separately and leave them to take their time.

DO LEAF BLOWERS SUCK?

They're undeniably effective, and if you need to move a huge quantity of leaves, which can be back-breaking work done manually, a leaf blower is usually the speediest and easiest way to do it. They're noisy, though, and not great for the environment – the petrol-powered ones especially – so keep their use to a minimum.

Q Can I have wildlife and a vegetable plot?

WILDLIFE CAN BE BOTH FRIEND AND FOE in the vegetable patch. No one wants slugs in their potatoes or onion fly targeting their garlic, but beetles, lacewings and ladybirds are all valued predators and should be welcome visitors. What's the best way to ensure balance in the vegetable garden?

Some susceptible crops are best netted – soft fruit, for example, usually needs to be protected from birds – or covered with an insect-proof mesh (there are meshes available that are fine enough to keep out even very small insects such as carrot fly).

Mixed up planting

Companion planting has had a bad rap over the last decade: the performance of many of the traditional pairings that were said to protect the crop and see off or distract pests wasn't necessarily proven in science. But mixing things up and putting small areas of a variety of plants together, rather than having a very large area of a single type of plant, does seem to help to deter the insects the vegetable gardener doesn't want and to encourage the ones you do. There's some evidence that insects first land on plants and only

A mixed approach usually works best. Depending on which crops you're growing, use physical barriers with other environmentally friendly answers, such as mixed planting and nematodes, and it should be possible to harvest your crops without disrupting the biodiversity you're trying hard to establish.

then decide whether they're the 'right' ones for their purposes (feeding or laying eggs), but that mixed planting seems to confuse them and slow down the eating or egg-laying process. This means that the old potager style of vegetable gardening, in which herbs and flowering plants are mixed in with crops, may make scientific as well as aesthetic sense.

Slug and snail damage can be exasperating for the gardener – one option is to conduct night-time slug hunts and pick them off by hand.

Devil's coach horse beetles (*Ocypus olens*) look like large black earwigs; both adults and larvae are enthusiastic predators of a wide range of species, including slugs.

Build a beetle bank

Many beetle species are useful predators in the vegetable bed. In agriculture, beetle banks are raised strips that run the full width of a cultivated field, with the aim of increasing biodiversity in farmed land. You can copy the idea in miniature in your garden by mounding up a ridge of soil 30–45cm (12–18in) high, then encourage grass to grow over it. The elevated height allows those beetles that prefer it to avoid the damp, and the grass offers cover during the day.

Try nematodes

Nematodes or eelworms are just some of the hordes of invisible life in the soil, but certain species can be used to target pests, such as carrot root fly, onion fly or slugs. A wide range of nematode 'fixes' are available commercially; follow the instructions carefully, as timing, soil temperature and moisture levels are all important for nematode treatment to be successful.

SLUGS IN THE VEGETABLE GARDEN

One nematode proven to be particularly effective against slugs is *Phasmarhabditis hermaphrodita*. Like other nematode treatments, it needs to be watered onto the soil, and ideally in two or three applications, rather than a single big hit, and it should be applied between spring and autumn. It's actually the bacteria contained within the nematode that kills the slug; it also seems to affect their pre-death behaviour, since infected slugs stay below the soil, and therefore nematodes have time to complete their own life cycle in the host body without the risk of larger predators, such as birds, eating the dead slug and bringing the nematode's operations to a halt. In other treatments (including banned pesticides) slugs are more likely to come to the soil surface to die. Some recent studies found that slugs will actively avoid areas where nematodes are present in the soil.

What's a Hugel heap (and do I need one)?

YOU MAY ALREADY HAVE HEARD the German term *Hugelkultur* (literally, hill culture) or listened to enthusiasts talking about its anglicized version, a Hugel heap. But what is it, and is it worth trying out from the wildlife point of view?

Once assembled and established, a Hugel heap doesn't need additional fertilizer; the buried wood keeps feeding it and, as it gradually breaks down, heats the heap and also causes slight movements in the soil around it which help to keep it aerated. The amount and type of wood used can vary, although it's essential that it is hardwood. You can use layers of branches or chopped lengths of larger branches or trunk, or indeed a whole tree trunk. The branch version may remain active and fertile for five years whereas the whole trunk 'heap' can go on working well for as long as 20 years.

How it works

As the German name implies, the typical form of a Hugel heap is a ridge: the wood is piled or stacked up into an inverted V-shape, covered with a thick layer of dead leaves, smaller branches and twigs, other plant trimmings and compost, and topped off with a layer of soil. Enthusiasts find that Hugel heaps are impressively fertile, producing excellent crops without needing much in the way of aftercare. They work best if the wood included at the centre is already beginning to rot. This is because the process of decomposition needs nitrogen, and wood that hasn't begun to decompose may remove a lot of nitrogen from the materials surrounding it, which may in turn reduce the heap's fertility in the first few years. Once rotting, the wood will start to release a range of nutrients and the heap around it should have good growing results from the start.

A Hugel heap is a mounded-up growing bed, used for edibles, piled over hardwood logs or sometimes a whole tree trunk, ideally wood that has already begun to rot. The gradually rotting wood will store water, provide a long-term, regular source of nutrients and warm the soil around it, while fostering numerous invertebrates, from beetles to woodlice. And you can plant both sides and top, maximizing the growing space.

HOW TO MAKE A HUGEL HEAP

If you want to try the technique for yourself (and unless you have a semi-rotting tree trunk ready to use), start on a fairly small scale.

You'll need:

• A selection of hardwood logs, preferably already beginning to rot down.

• Materials for the 'compost' layer of the heap. These can be a mixture of any or all of the following: garden compost, dead leaves, sticks and twigs, used straw pet bedding and shredded cardboard.

• Soil for the outer layer of the heap.

1 Choose a suitable spot for your heap. Ideally you need a flat plot. If possible, build it so that the finished heap will have one side in the sun and the other in partial shade, to suit a variety of different crops.

2 Pile up your logs into a stable, solid shape.

3 Pack the materials for the compost layer of the heap over and around the logs, pushing it into gaps. It should be at least 15cm (6in) deep, and it's fine to make it 30cm (12in) if you have enough material. Smooth it as best you can.

4 Add a layer of soil, around 15–20cm (6–8in) deep, as evenly as possible.

5 The heap is now ready for planting.

If a flatter bed is more convenient for planting, you can also make a Hugel structure without the heap. For this version, you dig a trench, fill it with wood surrounded by a compost layer, then simply lay a thick layer of soil on top.

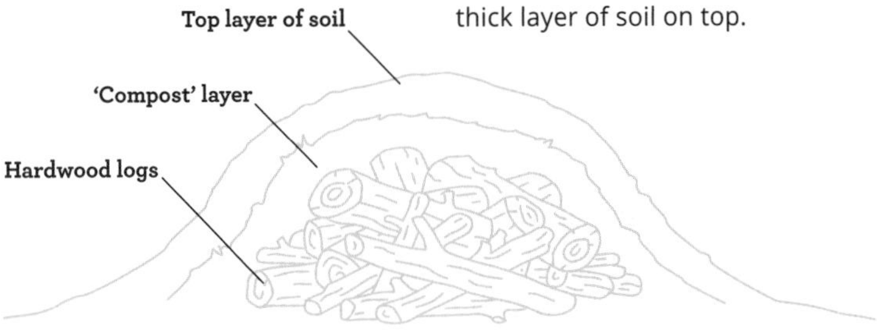

Top layer of soil

'Compost' layer

Hardwood logs

How many habitats can fit in my small garden?

One of the strengths of a garden when it comes to attracting wildlife is the opportunity it offers you to customize it for maximum appeal to a whole range of species. But how many habitats is it realistic to expect to create in a small urban garden?

There really isn't a limit. It's fine to think small when it comes to making habitats: after all, many of the species you're hoping to attract don't need a lot of space, just the right circumstances. And the more diverse you manage to make these mini-habitats, the more diverse the range of species you'll attract.

Toads and frogs spend the majority of their time away from the water. Outside the breeding season, they need plenty of options for cover on land.

Space to shelter, eat and sleep

If you define a habitat in terms of 'jungle', 'desert', 'savannah' and so on, it can be hard to see how it's going to apply to your garden. But if you look around with a wildlife eye, your garden already offers habitats and you can create more. Some parts of your plot may mimic similar conditions to those occurring in 'natural' habitats. If you have a boundary hedge, for example, it can offer wildlife some of the advantages of a woodland edge habitat, while an area of long grass is akin to natural grassland, and your compost heap has many of the

advantages of a woodland floor. You might have a wall covered in ivy offering both food and shelter for everything from birds to spiders, bees to butterflies, while a nice warm compost heap, even a small one, will appeal to a variety of beetles, millipedes, slugs and other mini-beasts who will both live and feed in it, and it will, in turn, become a feeding station for birds, frogs and possibly even slow worms or grass snakes.

A small patch of grass, left to grow long, will house plenty of bugs and insects and attract others who will come to feed. Even the smallest water feature, especially one with shallow sides and careful planting around it, offers another habitat to a whole host of species.

If you build it, they will come

As you add wildlife-friendly features, more wildlife will arrive, sometimes astonishingly fast: insects and birds don't have our earthbound problems with accessibility, and will be quick to spot desirable spots to rest and feed in from the air and to take advantage of them, even if they're located on a roof or a balcony or behind a high wall.

WHAT'S NEXT DOOR?

Wildlife isn't aware of property boundaries. Think in terms of adding habitats to those nearby, not just those within your own garden. If your neighbours have plenty of long grass, look at offering climbers, or planting a fruit tree or two; if there's a pond in the garden just over the hedge, think about creating a bog garden in your own patch. The more diverse the local offering, the greater the variety of species you'll attract.

The common spindle (*Euonymus europaeus*) is a small tree, common to woodland and hedgerows. Its berries are eaten by many species, and it's easily grown in your garden.

Who'll live in a stump?

WHEN A TREE HAS TO BE FELLED, the stump is often removed, burned out or treated with stump killer. This is a pity, since rotting tree stumps – provided they're not harbouring honey fungus, a killer of trees and shrubs – offer a very particular habitat that can appeal to some rare and extremely desirable species, such as stag beetles.

Left to itself, the stump of a newly felled tree will quickly play host to various recycling (saprophytic) fungi which will gradually begin to break the wood down. Once the stump has begun to decay, it becomes a powerful draw to creatures who dine on rotting wood; around 400 species of beetle may feed and breed there, including longhorn and click beetles. At the sizeable end of the beetle scale, at 7cm (2 3/4in) are the stag beetle (*Lucanus cervus*), the rhinoceros beetle (*Sinodendrom cylindricum*), which is around 2cm (3/4in) long with a single prong-shaped horn on its head and the lesser stag beetle (*Dorcus parallelipipedus*), an all-black species – both sexes look similar to the female stag beetle, but at around 3cm (1 1/4in) long, they're rather smaller.

Some species of beetle larvae live below the soil but dine on rotting wood. In traditional woodland the stumps of fallen trees supplied the combination naturally, but as woodland has become rarer, it's become harder to find. In a garden, the stump of a felled hardwood tree, left to rot without any chemical assistance, can offer the perfect habitat.

▶ Adult stag beetles (*Lucanus cervus*) are a rare but impressive sight: if you see one, treat it with respect and if it's somewhere exposed, transport it carefully to a safe spot nearby.

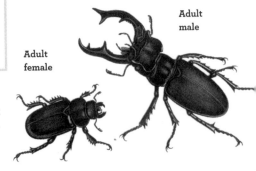

Adult male

Adult female

THE MAGNIFICENT STAG BEETLE

It's one of the most impressive insects found in Europe but sadly it's also highly endangered (it's already been declared extinct in Denmark and Latvia) – a long way from the 19th century when the French naturalist Jean-Henri Fabre wrote that on a single summer's evening he had caught enough stag beetles to fill his top hat. If you can offer a habitat either a wood pile part-buried in the soil or a rotting tree stump, there's a chance that you might attract the stag beetle (*Lucanus cervus*). In its adult form, the male of this huge black beetle has shiny brown wing cases and measures up to 9cm (3^1/2in), including the impressive antler-like jaws or mandibles from which its name is taken. (The all-black female is smaller – though still sizeable – and doesn't have the 'antlers'.)

Stag beetle enthusiasts need to be in it for the long haul: the unseen stages can last for between three and seven years before the adult beetles emerge for their brief moment of only a few weeks above ground. The female likes to lay her eggs underground, adjacent to rotting wood on which the larvae, once hatched, can feed. The larva simply eats, grows and moults. After the fourth moult, it buries itself in the soil or rotting stump and pupates, emerging as an adult beetle around three years later. Stag beetles don't eat as adults, although they may drink sap; the fat they accumulate as larvae sees them through their brief adult lives. Above ground, a male will take flight to find a mate; females tend to stick quite near their original 'nursery'.

If you're lucky, you may spot one of these impressive beetles in rather clumsy flight or on the ground (if the latter, only pick it up if it's directly in danger – ideally wearing gloves, as the adult female beetle can give you a painful nip; the male's jaws are weaker, but he may also bite).

Eggs

Larvae

Cocoon
and pupa
(female)

Pupa
(male)

Can I spray greenfly?

IN WARM WEATHER, greenfly seem to spread extraordinarily fast. Even if you generally avoid chemicals for the sake of your garden wildlife, is it okay to use a 'friendly' spray to get rid of them?

In a normal year, if you're patient, greenfly's natural predators – birds, hoverfly, lacewing and ladybird larvae, ladybird adults, parasitic wasps and various other species of beetle – will gradually bring the numbers down, although even the most aggressive predation won't eliminate them altogether.

APHID EXPLOSIONS

Patience and predators should work well enough in an average year, but what about those years when a mild winter followed by a warm spring boost aphid populations to plague levels? Avoid spraying with anything except water. Instead, run your finger and thumb gently down the afflicted shoots and stems to squash the aphids. You can also use a strong jet of water on stronger shoots: if the aphids are knocked off far enough they may well not return to the plant to do further damage.

If you change your view of greenfly from pests to valuable food source, you may learn to enjoy watching both ladybirds and their larvae, or lacewing or hoverfly larvae feast on them instead. If the problem seems to be spreading beyond their control, the most wildlife-friendly solution is to remove them by hand.

No-spray tactics

A spray that harms aphids will inevitably affect the insects that eat them. Even the mildest 'natural' soap spray can't distinguish between an aphid and a ladybird, which is why they're best avoided altogether. If you harm their predators, you run the risk that the aphids will stage an unchallenged comeback. They breed faster than anything else in the garden: their breeding pattern features something called 'telescoped generations', which means that each aphid contains young even before it's born – several generations in a single package.

Can I lure lizards?

NORTHERN EUROPE is at the northerly edge of viable lizard territory. Lizards are ectothermic, or cold-blooded, meaning that they must take their warmth from their environment, rather than being able to create it themselves, and are therefore more numerous in consistently warmer climates. If you'd like lizards in your garden, you need to offer them both the potential for warmth and plenty of cover.

Lizards like warm basking spots, a good cover of vegetation for concealment and water (they're capable swimmers). If you can offer a sunny wood pile, a bank, a dry stone wall or some flat stones, a patch of grass or thick foliage and perhaps a pond, you're doing what you can to encourage them into your garden.

Rather less decoratively, sheets of corrugated iron have proved particularly popular with both slow worms and common lizards (*Zootoca vivipara*). They shelter in the warmth underneath, so try to give up a quiet, sunny corner to a sheet laid directly on to the earth.

The UK has only three native lizards: the slow worm, the common lizard and the vanishingly rare sand lizard (*Lacerta agilis*) – which lives only in sandy heathland and natural dunes. Populations of a non-native, the wall lizard (*Podarcis muralis*, right), seems to be on the rise and it is increasingly seen in the south. The easiest way to tell them apart is that wall lizards are happy moving on vertical surfaces, while the common lizard tends to stick to level surfaces. Colour-wise, common lizards are brownish-grey and have orange or yellow bellies whereas wall lizards have a variety of colouring, but often have blue-green patches on their sides.

The warmth of the compost heap holds an obvious draw for lizards as well as other reptiles, but if you have a greenhouse that's also likely to appeal. If you spot one, leave well alone; it will be able to get in and out through the tiniest gaps, and there should be enough moisture and small prey to keep it healthy. It may even remove some pests from your plants. If you think lizards may be living in your greenhouse, avoid using chemicals: they are particularly susceptible to them.

Millipede or centipede: what's the difference?

ONE EATS ROTTING PLANT and animal matter and the other preys on small animals. One is much speedier than the other (it has to chase its food down). But can you tell which is which just by looking at them? And what are their respective roles in the garden?

Pill millipede,
Glomeris marginata

Despite having fewer legs to run around on, centipedes (members of the Chilopoda family) are predatory, and if you disturb one it will usually rush away at some speed. Millipedes (who belong to the Diplopoda family) respond more slowly and may freeze or curl up if you uncover one. Only some have the flat bodies that lead them to resemble centipedes: other millipede species resemble woodlice, and still others have round, curved bodies and look much more like grubs (although ones with lot of legs).

Which does what?

Centipedes are generally beneficial in the garden, eating a range of small micro beasts, some of them potential plant pests. Millipedes can do some damage to tender young leaves, but although they are sometimes found opportunistically eating around holes originally caused by slugs or snails, their jaws are not powerful enough to do much harm, and they more usually

If it will stay still long enough for you to count, there's one straightforward way to tell millipedes and centipedes apart (and there's a clue in the names): millipedes have two pairs of legs per body segment and centipedes just one.

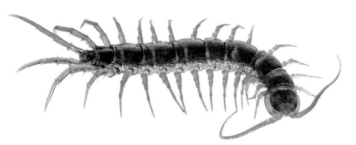

Stone/brown centipede,
Lithobius forficatus

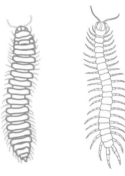

Millipede   **Centipede**

feed on decaying plant matter.
Both centipedes and millipedes
are nocturnal. During the day, they
hide in holes and corners around
the garden, but at night they come
out and either hunt or graze,
depending on which group they
belong to. Centipedes' sight isn't
good, so when they sense prey nearby,
they charge it and inject venom with
the poisonous claws, forcipules, at
the tips of their front legs.

Smooth movers

With so many legs, balance isn't
a problem for either group, but
coordination can be. Millipedes get
around this by operating the pairs of
legs independently; as one pair goes
down, the next pair goes up, allowing
their bodies to move in undulating
waves. Centipedes have a slightly
different arrangement: their legs
grow longer towards the end of their
bodies, which avoids the pairs literally
running into one another as the
centipede speeds up.

LEG COUNT

The centipede leg count
almost always falls short of the
100 its name implies, although
some species have far more.
The legs come in pairs, and the
total number of pairs is always
odd, from 15 all the way up to
177. Millipedes' legs, on the
other hand, come in even
numbers of pairs, totalling
between 20 and 200. The
number of legs isn't constant,
either: both groups lay eggs
and the young, when hatched,
look like miniatures of their
parents, taking several moults
to reach their adult size and
in some cases acquiring extra
segments, and the pairs of legs
that go with them, with each
moult. The legs are placed
differently on centipede and
millipede bodies: centipede's
legs are angled out and down
from their bodies, while the
legs of millipedes reach
straight down. The leggy
record breaker of the millipede
world is found in California:
with 750 pairs, the female of
the extremely rare *Illacme
plenipes* millipede has the
highest leg count of any animal
in the world.

How can I spot the microlife in my garden?

"A LIVING SPECK – the merest dab of life... is far more interesting to me than all the immensities of mere matter", wrote Jean-Henri Fabre, the great French naturalist of the 19th century. He was among the first to bring the extraordinary life stories of the tiny beasts – beetles, caterpillars, spiders and many more – found in his garden to a much wider public. He was right: up close, many garden creatures, even the tiny ones, are astounding. So what's the best way to watch them?

It's an engrossing hobby for anyone, but it's also a great way to introduce children to the charms of the natural world, watching wildlife on a tiny scale. If you start them young, there's the chance of sparking a lifelong interest in nature. Plus it can be a real-life distraction from the perils of too much screen time.

Where to look

You'll find invertebrates sheltering in long grass, on the leaves and stems of plants and shrubs, in and around flowering plants and on the ground itself. To start with, choose a likely spot (by the edge of a patch of long grass, at the base of a hedge, up close to a patch of ivy, by the side of a pond or by a brick path), sit very quietly and wait with your magnifying glass to watch

To start out, a magnifying glass and a field guide are all you need. As you become more used to observing, you'll want to collect a few specimens so that you can take a closer look. At this point, a sweep net, one or two collection trays, boxes and jars, plus a pooter for the actual collection will all prove useful.

what comes along. You may see black ants carrying dead insects far bigger than themselves, minute and parasitic bright red velvet mites riding on their much larger hosts, or youthful

Garden microlife, like this velvet mite (*Trombidium holosericeum*), is infinitely more interesting if you can look at it up close. Even insects you've regarded as pests can prove unexpectedly engrossing.

woodlice, much paler and pinker than their adult relations. Even everyday activities become engrossing to watch: why does the ant want that dead beetle? What's the relationship between that mite and its mount? How long before those baby woodlice develop their steel-grey adult armour?

Up close

To look at insects more closely, you'll need to collect them. A sweep net – a cane handle with a white bag-shaped net attached – works well brushed through long grass, while insects on leaves or stems can be shaken into a white net or tray (a pale-coloured

upturned umbrella also makes a very effective catch-all). To collect individuals from a surface – the ground, a tray or a net – an aspirator or pooter is an invaluable piece of kit. When you've had a proper look at your catch, release it (just shake it gently out of the container) near to where you originally picked it up.

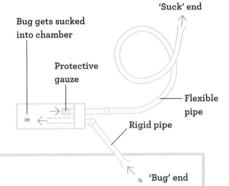

'Suck' end

Bug gets sucked into chamber

Protective gauze

Flexible pipe

Rigid pipe

'Bug' end

SUCK, DON'T BLOW

The 'pooter' was named after its inventor, William Poos, a US entomologist working in the 1920s. Although a simple tube aspirator for collecting insects had been invented towards the end of the 19th century, it was a very basic design. Poos's invention was a considerable improvement, consisting of a small airtight jar with two separate tubes inserted through the lid. One was long and flexible and the end within the jar was covered with a fine muslin, the other was shorter and rigid. To use it, you simply put the mouth of the rigid tube over the

insect you want to collect, put the end of the flexible tube in your mouth, and gently suck. The suction draws the insect up the rigid tube and into the jar, while the mesh stops you from swallowing the insect! It's a neat, easy-to-use design that's still used today.

However careful they are, professional entomologists still occasionally complain of 'Pooter's mouth' – the dry mouth resulting from an accumulation of extremely fine dust and debris that makes its way through the protective muslin – after long hours of sucking tiny lifeforms into the bottle.

Is my gravel wildlife-friendly?

GRAVEL CAN BE BOTH a practical and an attractive solution to certain situations. Maybe you need somewhere to park in a front garden but want to keep some growing areas, or perhaps you don't feel you have time to maintain a lawn-and-borders combination. But can gravel, whether over a small area or as a surface for a whole garden, be a good option for wildlife?

A gravel garden is also a great choice if you have free-draining sandy soil; the combination will favour drought-resistant plants – which are generally popular with pollinators – such as lavender, rosemary, euphorbias, marjoram,

A prepared area in a sunny spot, planted up with drought-tolerant plants, then overlaid with a layer of gravel, will attract a variety of invertebrates, from beetles to lacewings (above). Choose pollinator-friendly plants and lay gravel directly over the soil for the best results.

BROWNFIELD SITES

As far as wildlife is concerned, a gravel patch or garden can offer many of the benefits of brownfield site habitats. Land that has a history of human activity but that has been abandoned and unworked for a while may not always look especially attractive, but its mix of poor soil (provoking plants to flower hard to set seed) and areas of open ground (offering opportunities for basking, burrowing and hunting for different insect species) is often surprisingly rich in wildlife.

hebes, thymes, erigeron daisies and eryngiums. For the best wildlife habitat (and unless perennial weeds are a problem) avoid using a weed suppressant membrane between the soil and the gravel. Instead, prepare the bed first by digging and raking the soil, then plant it up before spreading the gravel directly on the earth, raking it around the plants. You'll need to water and weed regularly until the plants are established, for at least the first year, but after that a gravelled area doesn't need very much maintenance. Drought-resistant plants are often rich in both nectar and pollen.

Do I want this weird-looking worm?

YOU'RE WEEDING OR planting out seedlings when you find a very unfamiliar-looking worm underneath a pot. It's flat with wavy edges. It is an orange or purplish-brown colour with creamy edges and undersides. Is it just a worm or leech, and why haven't you seen anything like it before?

Your strange-looking worm is in fact a flatworm. There are several types. The three species of native flatworm are all small; but more likely, it's a species that has been accidentally imported from somewhere else and most of these pose a threat to native earthworms. Pick it up with a piece of damp tissue, transfer it to a bottle or box, and send it to the GB Non-Native Species Secretariat, a public agency for plant and animal health, to be identified.

The accidental importation of non-native flatworms is a problem. Most flatworms cross borders in the roots of container plants; often they're not unusual species in their country of origin, but they're previously unknown in their country of arrival – and they can be problematic when they do arrive. Just a couple of examples are the New Zealand flatworm (*Arthurdendyus triangulatus*) which grows up to 20cm (8in) long and whose diet is earthworms, and the Australian flatworm (*Australoplana sanguinea*) which can grow up to 8cm (3in) long and also dines on native earthworms. Both are widespread in the UK and parts of Europe and are considered a threat to biodiversity and soil health. The danger they pose to indigenous species of earthworm has a knock-on effect, as a scarcity of earthworms will in turn threaten the diet of many bird species.

What's the conscientious gardener's takeaway from this? That it's important to check the roots of any plants you bring into your garden carefully, whether they're from a nursery or plant merchant or are gifts from friends. And if you find a flat-looking worm, confine it in a box or jar and send it to be identified. You'll find the information you need at nonnativespecies.org.

New Zealand flatworm,
Arthurdendyus triangulatus

How can I incorporate a beetle-friendly log pile?

LOG PILES CAN COME IN MANY FORMS: large or small, designed or natural looking. What's the best type of wood? Where is the best place to site one? And is it possible to make a log pile attractive visually, as well as appealing to beetles and other invertebrates?

Practicalities first: if you don't already have a log pile, try to find the right wood to start one off. Hardwood logs – birch, ash, oak or beech – are the best choice, ideally at least 15cm (6in) in diameter, and with the bark still on them. A mix of woods is fine, but don't incorporate any slender prunings of willow as, unless long dead, they have a tendency to re-root and you may find yourself with an unwanted tree. Tree surgeons may be able to supply you with logs of a specific type if you have one in mind.

Think about the best site, which should be in either semi- or full shade. Hot sun will desiccate the wood and may not be conducive to the desirable growth of fungi; full shade will encourage fungi but may not offer

Log piles were originally just leftovers from tree felling, left to stand in a damp corner and duly proving irresistible to beetles and other feeders and breeders who appreciated rotting wood. But with a little planning, you can have a good-looking log pile that, as far as its inhabitants are concerned, provides exactly the same habitat.

a warm enough environment for some animals or insects. If you want to plant around and over it, a log pile backing onto a soil bank will make this easier. Log piles tend to look most natural with either trees or a hedge behind them, simply because this resembles their original habitat most closely.

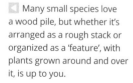

◁ Many small species love a wood pile, but whether it's arranged as a rough stack or organized as a 'feature', with plants grown around and over it, is up to you.

Old man's beard,
Clematis vitalba

Log pile aesthetics

When you've sourced the wood and found the right spot, think about what you want it to look like. Evenly piled, similar-sized logs of a fairly regular length will look neat and can be anchored by posts driven in at the corners. If you want a more organic effect, try varying diameters, perhaps with an uneven, undulating top line and gaps filled in with brushwood. If it's backed with soil, a planting of green euphorbias could make an appealing backdrop, or you can grow a climber over the heap itself. Old man's beard (*Clematis vitalba*), with its fluffy seed heads, looks particularly good scrambling over a wood pile. As the logs begin to rot down, small primroses and wood violets can also be planted in between the mosses which will have colonized naturally.

THE MESSY MYTH

One of the biggest myths propagated about the wildlife-friendly garden is that it needs to be untidy for maximum biodiversity. Gardeners are constantly urged to leave 'messy corners' to attract wildlife. While there's a grain of truth in this (many species do like piles of dead leaves, and many others will happily hide out in compost), wildlife is indifferent as to whether a leaf mound or log pile is neatly confined or a roughly arranged heap, or whether your compost is simply mounded up or tidily housed. All the wildlife sees is the right habitat, whether it's presented in a rough-and-ready or a carefully designed fashion. So if you're a gardener with a natural tendency to order, by all means stack your log piles neatly and make tidy chicken-wire containers for your leaf mould. If the conditions are right for them, you'll attract plenty of birds, bees and invertebrates – even if your borders are planted in straight lines.

Is no-dig best for wildlife?

IN THE PAST, traditional gardeners believed that thorough and regular turning of the soil was the best way to keep it aerated, weed-free and healthy. But in the 1970s and 1980s, a number of pioneers began to introduce the idea of a no-dig system – that is, adding thick layers of mulch to the soil without digging it in. Today, no-dig gardening has many enthusiasts in the context of plants, particularly for growing vegetables, but is it best when it comes to wildlife?

What about the worms?

The major argument for the no-dig system is that worms will do the work of mixing the mulch with the soil, enriching it and, in their tunnelling activities, aerating it, without human intervention. Worms are resilient: populations appear to remain healthy even in soil that is dug, so long as it also has a good proportion of organic matter. But no-dig principles ensure that all kinds of life near and on the

There's plenty of evidence to show that no-dig works well, although gardeners on very heavy clay soil may feel that worms cannot do all the work of introducing organic matter on their own, especially when soil is first brought into cultivation. When it comes to the health of the soil, no-dig is probably more beneficial to all kinds of soil life than the disruption of traditional digging.

OTHER WILDLIFE

Some larger species may appreciate the no-dig system, too. Toads, for example, often shelter in shallow burrows or hidey holes in the soil and can fall victim – sometimes literally – to enthusiastic digging. And traditional, thorough soil turn-over can also disrupt other valued inhabitants, such as beetles and bumblebees, who may inhabit the edges of growing areas in garden verges or banks.

surface of the soil remain undisturbed, allowing a honeycomb of tunnels and pockets – not just the tunnels and burrows of worms – to aerate the soil. In a no-dig vegetable garden, it's worth keeping working areas narrow enough to reach across from a path, as it's best not to compact your nicely aerated soil with repeated human trampling.

Are grubs good?

PERHAPS YOU'RE DIGGING or repotting and you find a C-shaped grub (or several). Obviously they're the larval stage of... something. But are they good or bad for your garden?

Chafer grub

There's a useful run-down on the five different forms larvae take in chapter 1 (see pp57). But the cream-coloured, C-shaped larvae you tend to find in or on soil may belong to a range of different species.

Chafer grubs

These are the larvae of chafer beetles. They vary in size, but all have distinct brown heads and C-shaped creamy-white bodies with three pairs of legs. Some are pretty big: the cockchafer grub can reach up to 5cm (2in) in length. Chafer grubs can do damage to roots of grass in the lawn or plants in the border, which is where they're most often found. Lawn enthusiasts will have to decide whether they can put up with the bare patches that can result from chafer damage; if you really can't, nematode treatments are the only way to deal with them.

Stag beetle grubs

You'll only find these around dead wood. If you do find some – they look similar to chafer grubs but can grow up to 11cm (4 ¼in) long – cover them up deeply and leave them alone.

Vine weevil grubs

Most commonly found around the roots of pot plants, these grubs have the distinct brown head and white C-shaped grub body but are legless and just 1cm (½in) long. They're not popular with most gardeners: a bad infestation will eat away a plant's roots and kill it. Timely nematode treatment (either watered in, or in the form of traps) is usually effective but may need several applications. With nematodes a successful result may be dependent on soil temperature.

A grub is the larval stage of an insect with a complete metamorphosis (those which have a pupal stage). The term can be used to describe the larvae of many insects, including caterpillars and maggots. And, like insects, you'll welcome some, while others – vine weevil grubs, for example – you won't. You'll find some clues to what you've got from where you find it.

What use are spiders?

IN AUTUMN, SPIDERS SUDDENLY SEEM TO PROLIFERATE: in the early morning their dewy webs are everywhere. But what part are they playing in the garden the rest of the time – and how many kinds are there?

Orb spiders, perched in their familiar webs, are probably the most familiar to us, but there are plenty of other species (around 650 in the UK alone), the great majority of which hunt down their food rather than spinning a web and waiting for it to come to them. All play a useful dual role in the garden, being both predators and prey.

Hunters

The iconic spider-in-a-web is most likely to be a female garden spider (*Araneus diadematus*), easily identified by the spotted white cross on its brown back (the males are much smaller). By late summer, when the spider is now fully mature and at maximum size, the webs become visibly larger, which is why spiders are suddenly so much more noticeable when September comes. Its 'classic' style of web is just one of five different types you may see around the garden, in shapes ranging from funnels to flat sheets.

Despite the familiarity of spiders' webs, far more species of spider in the garden catch their prey by actively (and sometimes stealthily) hunting it down without spinning a web at all. There are wolf spiders, who chase down their prey with incredible speed; pirate spiders, who mostly hunt down smaller spider species; woodlouse spiders, who lift an armoured woodlouse up with a sort of forklift motion, then pierce its soft underparts to inject venom; and the purseweb spider, who spins a thick cushion of web, waits under it until her prey sets foot on it, then quickly saws a hole through the web with her jaws and rushes up to snatch her victim. Some web spiders also have mugging techniques: *Zygiella x-notata*, another orb spider, leaves a radial section of the web unspun, with a single tightrope

Woodlouse spider,
Dysdera crocata

Missing sector
orb weaver,
*Zygiella
x-notata*

leading through it to nearby cover.
As soon as prey lands, the spider
charges along the 'rope' and grabs
it. And there's even the flower crab
spider, who has mastered the art
of ambush (see box).

What do they eat?

A huge range of small animals,
from aphids and flies to other
spiders and bees.

... and what eats them?

At the other end of the spectrum,
what hunts them? Spiders appear
on a lot of menus: birds, frogs, toads
and centipedes all eat them, as do
larger mammals, such as hedgehogs,
foxes and badgers.

AMBUSHING ARACHNIDS

The Misumena group, or the
flower crab spiders, are masters
of an unusual form of ambush.
They're found all over the world,
from Chile to China, but *Misumena
vatia* is the only species native
to the UK. It's a pale spider with
a colour ranging from white and
yellow to a delicate green and
a body around 1cm (^{1}/3in) long;
if you look carefully, you'll
sometimes see one sitting in the
heart of a rose or perching on
a daisy (generally, you'll spot a
female; the male is much smaller).
It lurks in or on flowers and
ambushes visiting pollinators,
first grabbing them with its
claw-like legs (hence the 'crab'
part of the name), then uses its
fangs to inject both venom and
digestive enzymes. The former
paralyses the prey, the latter turn
its inner organs to liquid so that
the spider can suck them out,
leaving just a skeletal husk behind.
It also has the chameleon-like
ability to match its colour to its
sheltering flower, although, as
studies show, uncamouflaged
spiders seem to have just as much
success hunting as those who
change colour. Scientists haven't
yet established why the
camouflage is useful.

A white flower crab spider
(*Misumena vatia*), lurking on a
daisy flower.

Chapter 3

Water in the Garden

Should my pond be pristine?

THE WATER IN A NEW POND started off clear but has developed an all-over bloom of scummy green algae. Why does this happen, what should you do about it and how clear should the water of a healthy wildlife pond be?

Algae doesn't look great and in extreme cases can deoxygenate the pond, which may be a problem for resident wildlife, but there are a number of ways to redress the balance.

Why does it happen?

Algae are very simple plants. When the word 'algae' is applied to pond scum or weed, it means a number of different species, which may simply turn the water green or appear as blanketweed, made up of hair-like lengths of filamentous algae.

Strong growths of algae happen because the pond water is too rich in nutrients. This may be the result of having been topped up with tap water (tap water contains dissolved nutrients, which promote algal growth), keeping fish in the pond,

As with every other aspect of a wildlife garden, maintaining pond water is all about balance. It won't ever – nor should it – look like the water in a swimming pool, but a lot of algae is usually a sign that the water is too rich in nutrients.

or because nutrients in the sediment have been disturbed when cleaning out the pond. Another cause can be when rain or irrigation cause fertilizers used elsewhere in the garden to run into the pond.

▼ You can fish a certain amount of blanket weed out, but unless you look for a long-term fix it will quickly reappear. Sadly many creatures can remain trapped in blanketweed even when left on the pond bank for a day or two before discarding.

THE BARLEY STRAW FIX

Barley straw helps to control the quantity of pond algae. If you're making up your own pad, stuff a bundle of straw loosely into a net or an old pair of tights, weight it with a stone (it needs to be heavy enough to be semi-submerged), and lay it on the surface of your pond. Trimmings from lavender hedges can also be added, as these seem to work, too. The contact with the water rots the straw which, as it decomposes, releases hydrogen peroxide, which inhibits the algae from making new growth. You need around 50g (2oz) of barley straw for each square metre (yard) of pool surface. It can take around six weeks to begin to take effect, so add it in early spring; once it starts, the results will last for around six months (the straw has done its job when it turns black, and should be removed). If you have a large pond, it's better to make several straw pads, rather than having a single outsize one, and spread them around.

Ponds that are sited in full sun, are uniformly shallow or have few plants in them, are all more susceptible to algal blooms, which are commonest in spells of sunny or hot weather.

How to fix it

When it comes to pond management, gently does it. Don't drain the pond and refill it, as this will start the whole cycle off again and won't help to 'balance' the water. Instead, float barley straw on the pond (see box) or add liquid barley-straw extract (sold online or in aquatic nurseries) to the water, following the instructions. Pulling thick masses of blanket weed out is only ever a temporary fix; if you do this, leave it on the side of the pond for a day to help any creatures brought out with it to escape back into the water. After this time, it can be composted.

In the long term, take measures to reduce further nutrient release into the water and introduce more floating and oxygenating plants into the pond: as a rule of thumb, these should take up around a third of both the surface and the underwater area of a wildlife pond. As wildlife arrives at a new pond, the numbers of creatures that eat the algae, such as water fleas, will increase.

Who's living at the bottom of the pond?

YOU MAY HAVE ALREADY SEEN a range of flying insects and spotted frogs or even newts in and around the pond, but which creatures will live full-time in your wildlife pond, and what kind of lives do they lead?

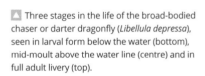

There's a long list of larvae that might live in a pond, those of mayflies, caddisflies, alderflies, some hoverflies, midges, dragonflies and damselflies among them. Other residents may include water snails, water beetles, water boatmen, leeches, plus plenty of detritivores, including water slaters (which look like and are related to woodlice) and small freshwater shrimps.

▲ Three stages in the life of the broad-bodied chaser or darter dragonfly (*Libellula depressa*), seen in larval form below the water (bottom), mid-moult above the water line (centre) and in full adult livery (top).

It's important for a pond to have shallow and gradually sloping sides to attract maximum wildlife diversity – to give a habitat to the many pond dwellers who prefer the shallows, and to allow those species that need access but don't live exclusively in the water to climb in and out easily. Fewer species live in the depths of the pond, where less oxygen is available. Frogs that have chosen to overwinter in the bottom of a pond and buried themselves in the silt layer breathe through their skin so still need to be near oxygenated water.

Pond dipping

If you want a close-up look at who's living in the pond, half fill a plastic bucket or large bowl (a pale colour will make it easier to spot small creatures) with pond water, then gently dip and pull a long-handled net through the pond, tip out the contents into the bucket and see what you have. Have a field guide and perhaps a magnifying glass – most of what you'll find will be quite small – at hand, and be careful when emptying the net into the bucket, so as not to crush your catch.

BRIEF LIVES

You're likely to have spotted mayflies (Ephemeroptera order) around your pond: they have very long tail filaments, which look like fine bristles extending from the end of the body, and when they land, you can see that the front pair of their wings is much larger than the back pair. You may have heard that mayflies emerge in their adult, winged form, mate and die, all within a day, but mayfly species are very numerous – there are 51 species in the UK and an estimated 369 across Europe – and their lifespans vary. One of the species most commonly found around ponds is the Pond Olive (*Cloeon dipterum*). Like most mayflies, the lion's share of its

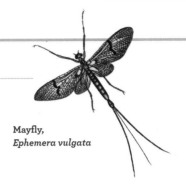

Mayfly,
Ephemera vulgata

life is lived as a larva, or nymph, underwater. Unusually, its eggs hatch as soon as they are laid, and the nymph (which, like the adult, has three long, fringed tail filaments), is found around the stems of underwater plants and in the shallows of the pond, feeding on algae. It can overwinter in the water, managing on very little oxygen, but it will crawl up a stem when it is ready to transform into an adult, where, like other mayfly species, it will go through a remarkable double moult – first shedding the larval case to reveal a sub-imago (or dun), which is rather drab in colour, then transforming again into its final adult form, the imago (or spinner), with glittering wings and a gleaming body. Unlike most mayflies, the female mayfly spinner doesn't mate immediately but flies off for up to two weeks, before finding a partner, mating, laying her eggs and dying shortly afterwards.

Pond olive adult

Pond olive nymph

How can I attract dragonflies to my garden?

WITH THEIR VIVID COLOURS, iridescent wings and, in some cases, their speed on the wing – certain dragonfly species have been recorded flying at over 30kph (20mph) – dragonflies (sub-order Anisoptera) and their smaller relatives, damselflies (sub-order Zygoptera) add some glamour to a pond environment. Are there any ways in which you can make your pond especially attractive to them?

Dragon or damsel?

Do you know which is which? There are around 30 species of the former and 21 of the latter to be found in the UK, but some are quite habitat specific, and not all will frequent ponds. It's quite easy to spot the difference between them when resting: dragonflies hold their wings out flat from their body, whereas damselflies perch with their wings folded up behind them.

Migrant hawker,
Aeshna mixta

Damselflies are also smaller and weaker in flight; up close, their eyes are clearly separated, while dragonflies' two eyes meet in the middle of their heads.

Both dragonflies and damselflies need a good supply of the small insects that make up their adult diet – midges, gnats, mosquitoes – and warm, sunny conditions for both hunting and roosting. Some species spend a lot of time perching and for them it's worth ensuring there are tall-stemmed plants (or simply tall stakes) that offer a good vantage point over your pond.

How dragonflies live

Dragon- and damselflies have similar life cycles. Both lay their eggs either near the water on plant stems or directly into it and, once hatched, spend their larval stages in the water. How long the insect spends as a larva varies widely: some damselflies have just two or three months as nymphs while species of dragonfly may last as long as five years in the nymph stage. All moult a number of times as larvae, but for their final moult, they climb out of the water onto a plant stem, shed their larval coats and, after an hour or

Banded demoiselle (male),
Calopteryx splendens

two, when their bodies and wings have hardened, are ready to fly. They then spend some days hunting, in the course of which they will take on their full adult colours, before moving back near water to mate. If you're lucky, you may see a pair in the act of mating, holding the shape known at the 'wheel'. The male moves sperm to a position under his thorax, then grips the female behind her head with a pair of claspers near the end of his abdomen. The female curls her own abdomen round to receive the sperm. In some species the position may be held for hours. Most dragon- and damselflies live just a couple of weeks as adults, although a few may last for as long as two months.

Who will visit?

If you can offer a sunny site, plant shelter around the shallows and plenty of good lookout perches, there are a number of species that may be attracted to your pond. Damselflies may be more frequent visitors if you have a small pond, while some dragonfly species are drawn to larger areas of water. Widespread damselfly species you may spot include the large red (*Pyrrhosoma nymphula*),

the azure (*Coenagrion puella*) and the blue-tailed (*Ischnura elegans*). Of the dragonflies, a selection of hawkers, chasers and darters all frequent ponds, and some are very territorial: you may see them swooping down from their perches to chase off others. It's worth keeping a field guide on hand to identify visitors.

WORLD TRAVELLERS

Despite their ethereal appearance, some species of dragonfly can travel great distances. One in particular, the aptly named globe skimmer (*Pantala flavescens*), undertakes a staggering migratory journey, starting in the state of Tamil Nadu in southern India, then crossing the Arabian Sea with stopovers in the Maldives and the Seychelles, before finally arriving in East Africa, a trip which adds up to around 18,000km (11,000 miles) and may take three or four generations of dragonflies to complete. And all this from an insect with a maximum wingspan of just 8.4cm (3in).

Are very small ponds still useful?

YOU'D LIKE A POND, but the only available space in your garden is very small – about 3m by 3m (10ft by 10ft). Is it worth making one, or will the wildlife benefits be negligible in such a tiny space?

Smaller ponds

If the small space you can spare is open soil, you can dig out and line a small pond in the same way that you would a larger one, although in such a small area your pond may have steeper sides than is ideal.

Alternatively, a container pond is a solution if you don't have access to soil to dig one in. You could use an old sink, a recycled plastic trug or bucket, or a wooden half-barrel, none of which will need lining provided that they are checked and found to be watertight. While there are some things this solution won't have – a container pond, for example, can't offer varying depths

and the shallow, sloping edges that are so desirable for wildlife – it will still attract some species, and if you customize it cleverly, you'll be able to maximize its appeal. Plant a few suitable border plants around one side of the mini-pond if it's sunk in the ground, or plant up some pots to cluster around a raised container pond. This will offer cover for frogs and other visitors, and you can choose one or two aquatic plants to float in the water, too (see box). Finally, fill your pond with rainwater and organize a 'ladder' on the inside and outside if necessary, made from a piece of wood or half-bricks or stones, to ensure that wildlife can easily climb in or out.

No pond is too small to be wildlife-friendly. Water in any form punches above its weight in a garden, and even the tiniest pond will make a pit stop for a variety of species, even if they don't all stay. In very limited spaces, it's worth giving some thought to the form your 'pond' should take.

Who'll visit?

Pond skaters and water beetles are often the first to turn up at a new pond and there will probably be plenty of tiny invertebrates amongst the floating plants' stems within a week or two; water snails in particular hitch a lift in the roots of water plants. Frogs may arrive within the first year and, if you're lucky, newts. Birds are likely to visit for a drink and a wash, too.

PLANTS FOR A SMALL POND

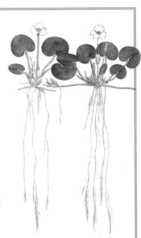

Plants for a container pond need to offer enough cover both in the water and around it without outgrowing their small-scale surroundings too fast. One floating plant, or two at most, will offer shelter in a pond around 1m (3ft) in diameter, and two or three marginal plants will give cover on the edges. Most marginals need very moist soil; if your garden can't deliver this, consider adding an inexpensive drip system alongside the container.

Floating:
Frogbit (*Hydrocharis morsus-ranae*) A pretty perennial (above right) with small white flowers and rounded leaves. It has a maximum spread of around 50cm (20in); you can pull bits off if it's growing too large.

Miniature water lily (*Nymphaea 'Pygmaea Helvola'*) A small water lily with a maximum spread of just 50cm (20in) but all the appeal of the larger versions: scented yellow flowers with bright orange stamens and round deep green leaves with purple blotches.

Shallows/marginal:
Water forget-me-not (*Myosotis scorpioides*) This perennial looks very like its border cousin, with small blue, yellow-centred flowers.

It can be planted in damp soil alongside the container pond or in a submerged mesh pot.

Marginal:
Green rush, dwarf rush (*Juncus ensifolius*) A small perennial rush that grows up to 50cm (20in) tall, with characteristic strap-shaped leaves and small mauvish-brown flowers in summer.

Lesser spearwort (*Ranunculus flammula*) Sprawling leaves growing in a loose clump up to 70cm (30in) across , and covered in bright-yellow buttercup flowers in early summer.

Will tap water harm wildlife?

OVER A DRY SPELL OF WEATHER water levels in a pond can drop quite sharply. If you don't have enough rainwater stored to top it up, is it safe to use tap water? Or will it affect the insects and other wildlife living in the water?

Tap water isn't ideal for a wildlife pond. Although it's treated to be safe for humans to drink, it usually contains chlorine and chlorinates and is much higher in nitrates and phosphates than rainwater. Adding it regularly or in large amounts to the pond can result in bumper growths of algae and a consequent lowering of oxygen levels in the water. Small amounts will do no harm.

Before you top up a wildlife pond, consider whether it's really necessary. Water levels in natural ponds go up and down, sometimes quite steeply, and the majority of species in a pond live around the plants in the shallows – often in just 5cm (2in) or less of water. While the less mobile wildlife wouldn't survive if the pond were to dry out completely, most species will be able to cope with a fall in water level, and it may be better than the pond being refilled with less-than-ideal water.

BE PREPARED

If you have plenty of saved rainwater on hand, the question of whether to use tap water or not needn't arise. If you don't already have a water butt, see if you can install one, even if it's fitted to a small structure such as a garden shed or greenhouse; if you do already have one, could you make room for another?

Can a wildlife pond have goldfish?

FIFTY YEARS AGO, every traditional garden pond had goldfish – today, it's no longer a given. But is there any real reason why you shouldn't include goldfish in your pond if you want them?

To some extent, how much fish predation goes on may depend on the size of the pond: a very large pond with shallow edges and plenty of dense plant cover may offer enough shelter for tadpoles and other creatures to survive the fish. And goldfish don't lack predators of their own: their presence may attract a heron to your garden – and if it does, the fish may not survive the visit! Taking the various factors into consideration, it's probably best to decide on either a goldfish pond or a wildlife pond. As neither needs to be large you could even opt for both if you have the space.

Goldfish are efficient top predators of tadpoles, eating smaller pond life including frog and newt tadpoles (toad tadpoles, on the other hand, are mildly toxic, and fish usually leave them alone). Goldfish faeces will also add nutrients to pond water, which may encourage an algae problem and increase the need for pond pumps and filters.

What about sticklebacks?

Sticklebacks, widely found in wild ponds and rivers, are sometimes suggested as alternatives to goldfish, but while these spiny little fish are fascinating in their own right, with elaborate breeding rituals including courtship dancing, they're also keen predators of everything from water fleas and insect larvae to tadpoles, so are best avoided if you want as many different species as possible in your pond.

▼ Even in urban surroundings, the grey heron (*Ardea cinerea*) will visit ponds regularly to prey on their inhabitants. As well as amphibians, herons can cope with quite sizeable goldfish, swallowing them in a couple of strong gulps.

Do honeybees bathe?

ON A WARM DAY you'll often see a honeybee drinking from the edge of a plant saucer that's filled with rainwater. Sometimes there'll be several of them. But do bees use the water for anything but drinking – do they actually bathe?

Honeybees don't take water baths in the way that birds do (although they sometimes have a dry wash, using the hairs on their legs like brushes to shed excess dirt and pollen). But in hot weather, in addition to drinking water, they collect it to take back to the hive where it will be used to keep the interior cool, as well as for the other bees to drink.

Collecting nectar and pollen is thirsty work; on a hot day you may spot bees lining up to drink from any available water source.

It's estimated that a honeybee hive at peak population in midsummer may need anything between 1l and 4l (2–8pt) per day – even with a healthy population of worker bees, that's a lot to collect. Worker bees save the water in their crops, regurgitating it when they get back to the hive, where it is used in several different ways to keep the colony working. Once they've found a water source that they like, the workers from a hive may visit it in great numbers. There's some evidence that they leave pheromone 'markers' to help their hive colleagues to locate water and they may also perform a 'waggle dance': the ritual in which worker bees perform a sequence of moves to guide their fellow workers to good resources, usually rich sources of pollen and nectar, but in hot weather, water.

PUT OUT A BEE DRINKER

Every garden, however tiny, has space for a bee drinker in hot summer weather, and it will be used by bumblebees, wasps and possibly other insects as well as honeybees. Honeybees can drink and collect water to take away, and do both safely; in deeper water, without a secure foothold, they can sometimes drown. The drinker should ideally be filled with rainwater, so you'll either need to have access to a water butt or to leave a bucket out to collect it.

1 Take a wide, shallow dish or plant saucer and half fill with marbles, gravel or small pebbles, rinsed in water.

2 Spread the stones out across the bottom, leaving a slight hill in the middle.

3 Half fill the container with rainwater so that some gravel in the centre is dry, and the rest is semi-submerged, then put it outside in semi-shade and see who turns up to drink from it.

Remember to clean and refill the drinker once a week. Top up daily in hot weather.

Marbles/gravel/pebbles   Dry mound   Rainwater

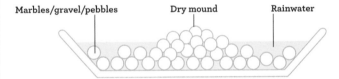

What happens to water in the hive?

First, worker bees give water directly to the nursing bees. The latter feed bee larvae with a jelly-like substance made from a mixture of pollen, nectar and water. The jelly varies in consistency according to how old the larva is, with the younger larvae needing a more liquid diet; if the nursing bee is short of water, the jelly won't be runny enough. Second, they cool the cells containing larvae or baby bees by spreading a thin film of water on top of each cell, then energetically fan it with their wings, causing the water to evaporate and bring the overall temperature down. And third, they use it to water down the texture of stored honey that can't be used as food because it has crystallized.

Can I import wildlife to my pond?

NEW OWNERS SOMETIMES WANT to hurry things along a little – particularly if there's plenty of frogspawn in a neighbour's pond and there isn't any in yours. Is it okay to collect some in a bucket and import it? Or maybe there's some fertile-looking mud in a nearby stream? Will a bucket of that help to boost the invertebrate population?

Don't do it. This is one of the risks just not worth taking in a wildlife garden: you don't know what you're importing, and different habitats, even when they're located near to one another, may have quite different conditions. You may accidentally bring in unsuitable species – plant or animal – or disease.

You can't know what you're importing in mud, and amphibians in particular suffer from a number of conditions that affect their health and that aren't, as yet, well understood. A big part of the joy of setting up a wildlife pond is watching it gradually come to life as creatures discover it for themselves. If you offer frogs a congenial habitat, they'll turn up in time – usually within a year – as will plenty of other species, from damselflies to water fleas.

FROM NO FROGS TO 'TOO MUCH' SPAWN

When they do make an appearance, frogs can produce an astounding quantity of frogspawn, to the point where less experienced pond owners sometimes query whether they should scoop some out to give the rest a chance. There's no need: although a female frog can produce literally thousands of eggs and a fair number may make it as far as hatching, you're unlikely to end up with too many adult frogs. Both frogspawn and tadpoles are popular with a lot of predators, such as dragonfly larvae, and the vast amount of spawn is to ensure that at least some eggs will make it through to adulthood.

Do ponds need pumps?

Many old-school gardeners maintained that a pond must have a pump in order to keep the water clean. But does a pump have any place in a wildlife pond?

Ornamental goldfish or koi carp ponds do need a pump because fish produce a lot of waste which is high in nutrients. A pond managed for wildlife is best without fish and – without the nutrients that fish waste adds to the water – shouldn't need either pumps or filters.

Great diving beetle,
Dytiscus marginalis

The majority of owners of today's wildlife ponds opt not to have fish because they eat other valued species, such as tadpoles. Without them, and with plenty of oxygenating plants, most ponds achieve a balance in which the water is sufficiently oxygenated without the added help of a pump. While pumps with filters keep algae levels down (making the water appear clean), they can suck tadpoles and even young newts into the system; so if you do use a pump, to run a water feature, for example, be sure to fit a filter case with a wildlife protection system.

Portable oxygen

Life underwater is dependent on at least some level of oxygen, but some pond dwellers carry their own supplies with them. Adult diving beetles, for example, trap a bubble of air in a special cavity under their elytra (wing cases), which they use as an oxygen tank when they're underwater, taking oxygen through their spiracles, which are located on top of the abdomen. The beetle dives down into the water to hunt for food, and when the 'tank' is exhausted, returns to the water's surface to replenish supplies. Diving beetles have several other modifications to make life underwater easier: their hind legs are covered in lines of bristly hairs, for example, which increase their surface area and enable the beetle to use them as paddles.

Can I have a bog garden without a pond?

MAYBE YOU HAVE SMALL CHILDREN and are worried about the safety aspects of a pond, or perhaps you've always liked the idea of a bog garden. But do you need the marshy edges around a pond to make a natural bog garden, or can you create it as an individual, distinct habitat?

In terms of construction, a bog garden is similar to (but even simpler than) a pond: it's an area that is consistently damp but without open water. A semi-shaded site is ideal; full sun may call for frequent water top-ups, and full shade is less flexible when it comes to planting. There are one or two key differences from a pond when you're making a bog garden: first, while a hole in the pond liner is a big problem for a pond, you deliberately make a few evenly spaced holes in the liner for a bog garden (spiking it with a fork is the easiest way). And second, when you dig out the area you've chosen for a bog garden, there's no need to create the various different 'shelved' levels as you would for a pond. You're aiming to dig out to a depth of 20–30cm (8–12in), then line the base with a pond liner followed by a layer of gravel, topped off with a layer of soil with a proportion of leaf mould – which will help with water retention – mixed in.

It's as straightforward to make a bog garden as it is to create a pond and it will have plenty of appeal to wildlife in its own right. Not only is it a useful habitat for amphibians and damp-loving invertebrates, but with well-chosen plants it can also be valuable to pollinators – and pretty, too.

Purple loosestrife (*Lythrum salicaria*) is a great choice for a bog garden: it's colourful and popular with pollinators, and is also tolerant if the ground in which it's sited sometimes dries out.

FIVE GOOD PLANTS FOR A BOG GARDEN

Aim for a good range of heights and flowering seasons, to maximize your bog garden's appeal to pollinators while ensuring it offers plenty of shelter for ground dwellers.

Water avens (*Geum rivale*) A lovely clump-forming perennial with scalloped deep-green leaves and copious nodding pinkish-orange flowers in late spring to early summer. Very popular with pollinators. Maximum height 60cm (24in).

Yellow flag (*Iris pseudacorus*) The classic bog plant (right), hardy and tough, and quick to spread – you may need to separate the clumps every two or three years. Bright yellow iris flowers in spring and early summer. Maximum height 1.5m (5ft).

Marsh marigold (*Caltha palustris*) Grows in a clump, with large heart-shaped leaves and bright yellow buttercup-like flowers in spring. This plant is happy in sun or shade and popular with insects. Maximum height 40cm (16in).

Purple loosestrife (*Lythrum salicaria*) Popular with pollinators, with deep purple flower spikes in mid to late summer. Fairly shade-tolerant and will survive drier spells. Maximum height 1.2m (4ft).

Gypsywort (*Lycopus europaeus*) A nettle-like plant (left) with leaves growing in whorls, which has small white flowers with purple blotches in late summer. Although it's not particularly striking, gypsywort is unfussy and seems particularly popular with a lot of the smaller insect species. Maximum height 1m (3ft).

Does my garden offer enough food and shelter for frogs?

IF YOUR GARDEN IS ALL-ROUND WILDLIFE FRIENDLY, you've probably had sightings of frogs and toads, even if you don't have a pond. At times of year when they're not breeding, toads in particular can often be found quite a long way from water. But where do they actually live, what do they live on and how do they spend their time?

From water to land

Frogs breed in water because their eggs don't have a protective shell like those of reptiles; if they were left on land, they'd dry out without hatching. But adult frogs don't spend very much time there. Mating and egg-laying takes place in the course of a furious two or three days of activity in any shallow water – if a stream, pool or pond isn't available, a puddle may be pressed into service. Toads spend a little longer in the water at breeding season, but still not very long – at most, perhaps a couple of weeks. For the remaining 50 weeks or so of the year frogs and toads live elsewhere. And while frogs may sometimes go into their winter dormancy at the

Like most amphibians, frogs need water to breed in, as do toads (and newts). But the common frog (*Rana temporaria*) and the common toad (*Bufo bufo*) need spaces to hunt and hide in when they're on land, because this is actually where they spend about nine-tenths of their lives.

bottom of your pond, provided there is still some oxygen to be had, it's actually far more usual for them to overwinter on land, in heaps of leaf litter, in soily depressions under a pile of dead wood or rocks, or even in compost heaps: anywhere that is cool and damp and where they're unlikely to be disturbed. Toads will scrape

Young tadpoles eat algae but they turn carnivorous as they grow, dining on tiny pond creatures. As adults, frogs are unfussy eaters, tackling insects, worms, slugs and even snails with enthusiasm.

SECRETS OF SALIVA

Watching a frog catch its prey is impressive even if you don't know the mechanics of how it works. The mechanics, though, are really engrossing. Unlike mammalian tongues, a frog's tongue is attached at the front rather than the back of its mouth. It is also very long (around a third of the length of the frog's body) and very, very soft. This means that when the tongue shoots out of the mouth to catch an insect, it can more than double its 'resting' width, wrapping around its prey like a thin, flexible sheet. The whole manoeuvre takes a fraction of a second: a frog can fasten on an insect in a tenth of the time it would take you to blink.

A study at the University of Georgia in 2017 established that the frog's true secret weapon is its saliva, which can change texture in a moment, from thick and sticky to thin and runny. As the tongue strikes the frog's prey, the saliva coating becomes more liquid, surrounding the insect with a thin layer of tacky spit. But as the tongue begins to retract into the mouth, the saliva thickens. Having captured the insect, it's now holding it fast for the return journey. And once the meal is back in its mouth, the frog performs a final step to get it off its tongue and into its digestive system: it pops its eyeballs back into its head and uses them to push the prey off its tongue and down its throat. That's what's happening when you see a frog blink as it swallows.

---

out burrows for themselves in quiet corners. Neither frogs or toads really need 'houses': they're flexible when it comes to accommodation and are good at scoping out suitable shelter for themselves. Creating a 'cairn' of piled-up stones, or leaving small log piles in quiet corners, will ensure your garden has frog or toad appeal. Both amphibians are largely nocturnal, tending to hunt at night and rest during the day.

What frogs like

Freshly hatched tadpoles are vegetarians: they start their lives feeding off algae in the shallows of a pond or stream. But as they grow, they start to hunt, beginning with tiny pond-dwellers. By the time they've completely metamorphosed into young frogs – at around four months – they've become voracious predators. As adults they catch a varied diet of flies, worms, snails and slugs.

Which pond-side plants are most wildlife-friendly?

WHEN YOU'VE CHOSEN THE PLANTS that you would like to grow in your pond, what are the best choices for those that will grow around the edges? Apart from the aesthetic considerations – you'll probably want to mask the edges of the pond liner if you have one, and to make the pond look 'natural' – what considerations are there for wildlife?

Manage grass edges

If your pond was installed into a lawn, you probably cut up the turf and may have relaid at least some of it directly over the liner, so that it masked the edge and went down right to the water's edge. A word of caution here – if your pond is even partially bordered with grass that is actually in contact with the water, the turf may act as a wick in hot weather and can draw

Greater spearwort,
Ranunculus lingua

large amounts of water out of a pond surprisingly quickly. Conversely, in very wet weather, water may drain off the grass into the pond, bringing nutrients that disrupt the pond water's balance with it. You can easily avoid both these situations by banking up the soil at the edge of the pond to create a shallow divider, around 4–5cm (2in) high, between the water and the grass edge.

Which plants?

Pond purists may feel that they only want plants that would naturally occur around pond margins. And there's an extensive and attractive range of plants which are native to the UK and much of Europe; just a few examples include meadowsweet (*Filipendula ulmaria*), greater spearwort (*Ranunculus lingua*), water mint (*Mentha aquatica*), purple loosestrife (*Lythrum salicaria*),

Plants around the pond need to offer cover for small species coming to and fro on foot, including young amphibians making their first exit from the water, as well as stems that will support damsel- or dragonfly larvae as they emerge for their final transformation into adults. They should also be the right scale for your pond.

LEAVE IT TO NATURE?

There's one school of thought that says there's no need to plant up the edges of your pond at all, but recommends that you simply leave some unplanted margin and wait for the plants that will arrive naturally to grow. Not only will this happen surprisingly fast, but enthusiasts argue that there's also evidence that a brand-new pond is a habitat that's distinct even from the same pond once it's established, and as such may appeal to both flora and fauna which prefer a bare canvas, habitat-wise.

The case against leaving nature to get on with it is that it will not give instant visual appeal and you may find that less desirable plant species, such as docks, colonize first. If you're not sure which route to take, plant up some of your pond margin but leave a section bare and unplanted, and see what flora moves in.

flowering rush (*Butomus umbellatus*) and greater pond sedge (*Carex riparia*). But around a garden pond's edge it would be appropriate to include a few non-natives that will offer plenty of cover and insect-appeal, such as irises (*Iris ensata* and the smaller *Iris sibirica*, for example), lobelia (*Lobelia cardinalis*) and Bowles' golden sedge (*Carex elata* 'Aurea'), a smallish sedge that lives up to its name with strappy bright golden leaves.

**Purple loosestrife,
*Lythrum salicaria***

Think about scale

Do take size into account: very tall or vigorous marginal plants can quickly overwhelm a small pond, and a few 'classic' pond plants, such as bulrushes (*Typha angustifolia*) or branched bur reed (*Sparganium erectum*) look good but grow very fast and vigorously and will need regular cutting back if you want to include them (they also have the potential to puncture pond liners if left too long to their own devices). If you don't want to do too much plant management, choose plants that won't demand it.

Can I have water lilies?

INSTANTLY RECOGNIZABLE with their round leaves and glamorous flowers in colours ranging from pure white to subtle or vivid yellows through to pinks and deep reds, water lilies are a must-have for many wildlife pond owners. It is true that there's a suitable water lily for any pond, whatever its size and siting, or are some situations not right for them?

European white water lily, *Nymphaea alba*

Wildlife pluses

Water lilies combine the benefits of offering plenty of shelter for pond life below the water surface and flowers that pollinators love above it. If your pond has a sunny site (water lilies prefer at least four hours of sun per day), you simply need to decide which water lily or -lilies will suit its size best.

Planting water lilies

Unlike floating plants, water lilies have floating leaves but are rooted in the pond, either into the sediment at the bottom or into aquatic plant baskets that you've placed at their preferred water level. When you're choosing the best lily for your pond, you need to look at how much surface they'll eventually cover and their preferred depth of water. New water lilies that aren't yet fully grown are best planted in aquatic baskets filled with aquatic plant medium, which you can buy online or at an aquatic plant nursery. Once planted, the water lily can be

Water lilies like sun and still water: they won't do well near running water, such as a fountain, or in a very shady pond where, even if they grow, they're likely to produce foliage but no flowers. They'll work in different depths of water, and in terms of size they grow happily in any body of water, from a container pond to a lake.

placed in the pond with the leaves floating on the surface and the basket placed on an appropriate ledge in the pond, or, if necessary, raised on bricks. As the stems grow the basket can be lowered in the pond to accommodate them. When it's fully grown you may have to move your water lily into a bigger basket; one sign that a lily has outgrown its basket or is in water too shallow for it, is that the leaves no longer lie flat on the water, but instead push up above the surface.

WHICH WATER LILY?

Here are some of the most attractive options for ponds, according to their size. The dwarf varieties are small enough for container ponds; the large water lilies need deep water and a large surface space to accommodate their spread.

Dwarf or small water lilies that grow in water 30–45cm (12–18in) deep:
Nymphaea 'Pygmaea Rubra' Maximum spread 0.5m (20in), purple-blotched leaves and scented flowers that are deep pink on opening then gradually darken to a dark red.

Nymphaea 'Pygmaea Helvola' Maximum spread 0.5m (20in). Similar to Pygmaea Rubra, but with bright yellow flowers and orange stamens.

Medium-sized water lilies that grow in water 45–75cm (18–30in) deep:
Nymphaea 'Paul Hariot' Maximum spread 1.2m (4ft), with purple-blotched leaves and flowers that start the season a yellow-cream colour but deepen to orange-pink over time.

Nymphaea 'James Brydon' Maximum spread 1.2m (4ft), with purple leaves and bright pinkish-red flowers from early summer to autumn. Can cope with partial shade.

Large water lilies that grow in water 75–120cm (2½–4ft) deep:
Nymphaea 'Gladstoniana' Maximum spread of 3m (10ft) or more, with shiny green wavy-edged leaves and huge white flowers, up to 30cm (12in) across, with golden stamens.

Nymphaea 'Escarboucle' An old variety, with a maximum spread of 2.5m (8ft). It has beautiful scented, deep pinkish-red flowers with bright yellow stamens.

Does a wildlife pond need different depths?

YOU HEAR A LOT about 'ledges' and 'shallows' in wildlife ponds. Are they really necessary and if so, why?

How deep should it be?

Most sources recommend that a medium-sized garden pond – measuring perhaps 2 x 2m (7 x 7ft) – should go from shallow, very gradually sloping edges, perhaps 5cm (2in) deep, to around 60cm (2ft) at its deepest part. The deeper area protects wildlife during extremes of cold or hot weather, acts as shelter for hibernating amphibians and offers underwater cover when small pond life needs to shelter from predators. Unless you live in an area with much colder than average winters, or your pond is in a relatively shady site, you could opt for

Every good wildlife pond should have a gradual 'beach' slope on at least one side, to allow wildlife an easy route in and out of the water and to offer a suitable habitat for the many species who spend most of their time in the shallows. Ledges, as opposed to slopes, are introduced to give baskets (for underwater plants) a flat surface to stand on.

a shallow 'deep' point of somewhere between 30 and 45cm (12–18in); shallower ponds warm up faster in spring, which is better for most of the wildlife living in them. From the wildlife point of view, around half the area of the pond should ideally consist of shallow water, between 5 and 15cm (2–5in).

▼ Shallow edges and a few different levels in a pond will ensure that it offers an appealing habitat to the greatest possible number of species.

Sloping sides

Summer water level

Winter water level

Offer extra little pools/ trenches of water at the edges if you can

Rocks/marginal plants for shelter

Ledge for container plants

45–60cm (18–24in)

A hardwood branch for shelter and algal growth

WHAT THE TERMS MEAN

Plants for ponds and their surroundings have a terminology that can be confusing, from 'aquatics' and 'oxygenators' to 'emergents' and 'marginals'. What do they mean, and is there any overlap between them?

Aquatic plants
An aquatic plant is any plant that grows in water.

Oxygenating or submergent plants
An oxygenating plant is an aquatic plant, usually one fully submerged in water, hence the term submergent. During daylight hours it absorbs carbon dioxide from the water and releases oxygen into it. The category includes both bottom-rooted and free-floating plants without anchored roots (the latter are usually classified as floating plants). Check the label or with the nursery as to whether your oxygenator is best simply placed loose into your pond in bunches or planted into a basket.

Emergent plants
Plants that are rooted in the water with upright stems or leaves that emerge above the surface. There is some overlap between marginal and emergent plants.

Marginal plants
A marginal plant is one that grows at the water's edge, usually with its roots in the water and its foliage above it. Many will be happy in wet mud.

Bog or marshland plants
These are named for their natural wetland habitats. They grow near water; some will tolerate their roots drying out for brief periods in dry weather but generally require year-round damp soil.

Ledges
The only reason for your pond to have ledges rather than slopes is to give you somewhere to stand containers of pond plants. Containers are used for pond plants to enable them to grow in an artificial environment at a depth that suits them when there may not be much available material for them to root into. If you're creating a new pond, make a single wide ledge rather than one or more narrow ones: it will make it much easier to group underwater containers to get an appealingly natural look, while a narrow ledge may force you to line them up like soldiers.

Do birds need to bathe?

YOU'VE OFTEN SEEN BIRDS BATHING as well as drinking in
your garden, but they seem to do so even more frequently in very
cold weather. Are they just washing off dirt, or does the bathing
have an additional purpose?

Clean feathers make warm birds

A bird's feathers lead quite a tough
life. The barbules which make up the
flexible sides of every feather work
like tiny zippers: when they fall out
of alignment, it creates gaps in the
feather's edges. Birds use their beaks
to 'zip' them back up again. The downy
layer of feathers next to a bird's skin
can be puffed up to trap warm air
around its body in cold weather and
clean feathers that are free of dirt and
neatly aligned will keep the bird warm
more effectively. Clean, groomed
feathers may also affect how precisely
birds fly. One study by Newcastle
University in 2009 found that starlings
given the opportunity to bathe

The combination of regular
baths and preening is the way
that birds maintain their
feathers in top condition which,
in turn, ensures that they can
both fly efficiently and regulate
their body temperature,
keeping warm in cold weather
and cool when it's hot.

whenever they wanted could negotiate
an obstacle course consisting of
vertically hung string more accurately
than those prevented from bathing
for three days.

How you can help

Birds can take baths in puddles and
ponds, but if you place a custom-made
bird bath within sight of a window,
you'll be able to watch the whole
process of bathing and grooming.
It's important to clean the bath
regularly, scrubbing out dirt and

◀ Clean feathers make
for healthy birds, and wet
feathers are easier for a bird
to preen, oil and return to
perfect flying order.

WHAT ARE BIRDS DOING WHEN THEY PREEN?

A preening bird is looking after its feathers. After washing (damp feathers are easier to preen), it will take some oil on to its beak – the former is secreted by the uropygial, or preen, gland located under its tail – and work through all its feathers carefully, cleaning them, working outwards from the quill, arranging and aligning them, and rubbing small quantities of oil on them to maintain them in good, waterproof order. They also use the process to pick out mites and other pests from their plumage, and to strip out the tough coating of any newly grown feathers and manipulate them into the best position. It's a meticulous, thorough process which is enjoyable to watch.

Although most birds have preen glands some, including owls, hawks, pigeons and parrots, don't. You may have noticed that wood pigeons leave a fine white, dusty substance on the surface of the water after bathing in your pond or bird bath. This is called feather dust; it's a waxy powder made from the brittle ends of the pigeons' down feathers, which crumble when the bird combs through them with its beak. It's used in the same way as the oil from a preen gland, to groom the outer feathers and reinforce their waterproof finish.

European goldfinch,
Carduelis carduelis

algae and rinsing well so that there's no residue of cleaning materials left. This makes sure that it won't pass any avian diseases between birds. There's some evidence that birds prefer moving or splashing water (circulating water will stay cleaner as it won't suffer from algae build up), so if you decide to install a bubble fountain with a pump, although it will cost more than the most basic bird-bath model, you may benefit from even more visitors.

What about drinking?

Birds, of course, will use the bird bath to drink from as well as to bathe in, and up close you may notice that they drink in different ways. The majority of smaller garden birds dip their beaks, fill them with water, then throw back their heads to swallow it down. Pigeons and doves, unusually, can suck up water through their beaks and swallow it without having to enlist gravity by throwing their heads back to get the water down.

Will a pond be high maintenance?

IF YOU'RE A FIRST-TIME WILDLIFE POND OWNER, you may have wondered how much upkeep it will take. When a pond and its surroundings are set up, how much maintenance will it need?

Pond-watching

A pond that has a good structure and enough light will largely maintain itself. And gardeners with a wildlife pond usually spend a lot of time watching it for pleasure, observing the comings and goings of all kinds of species, from the mini-beasts in the water to the larger, more eye-catching visitors around it, which means that you'll be alerted early to everyday problems, such as blanketweed getting out of hand, an extreme drop in water level, sludge in the floor of the pond getting too deep or specific pond plants starting a takeover bid. A seasonal review should be plenty to keep it in good order: cutting back, dividing or moving plants as necessary; pulling out dead stems from water lilies and marginals in autumn; using barley straw as a long-term reducer of algae or, occasionally (and gently), cleaning out some of the mud at the bottom of the pond; or, in extremely dry weather, topping up the level a little with buckets of rainwater.

Spotting undesirables

The majority of non-native plants will work perfectly well in a pond, but there are a handful which are immensely invasive when they've escaped and established themselves in the wild. While they're no longer sold commercially, they were often passed from one pond owner to another. They can be managed in ponds, but they must be kept out of the wild. If you're getting rid of it such a plant, you must carefully remove it from the pond, let it dry out at the pond's edge, then compost, bury or burn it. Never dump it in general rubbish or outside the garden in another pond, stream or water course.

Once a pond is established, it needs keeping an eye on, rather than any elaborate maintenance schedule, and this shouldn't take much time. As its caretaker, you're trying to mimic a natural habitat and ensure that the various factors that affect it stay in balance, which may call for occasional intervention.

Great pond snail,
Lymnaea stagnalis

PLANTS TO AVOID LIKE THE PLAGUE

These are the top five plants that you don't want to introduce to your pond and which, if you have them and decide you don't want them, you must dispose of responsibly (be aware that they can regrow from just a tiny fragment of the original plant). If you're not certain what you have, check online identification guides.

New Zealand pygmy weed (*Crassula helmsii*) Introduced as an oxygenating plant for domestic ponds in the early 20th century, this tough little plant is frost resistant. It has vivid green foliage, with small narrow leaves and white flowers in summer. In the wild it will smother other species. It can grow both underwater and alongside water.

Parrot's feather (*Myriophyllum aquaticum*) A South American native which was introduced to Europe and the UK in the mid-19th century. It has feathery, multi-leaved stems which grow both under the surface and emerging from the water. It can survive dry spells. In the wild it can block waterways with fast-growing, thick 'rafts' of foliage.

Water-primrose (*Ludwigia grandiflora*) With a yellow flower (pictured), this was originally introduced as an ornamental water and bank plant. Hailing from South America, it has proved problematic in Europe and the UK, with the vigour to out-compete most other plants.

Water fern (*Azolla filiculoides*) Also known as fairy fern, the tiny leaves of this plant look inoffensive, but it's an extremely speedy grower and will quickly take over. Its thick carpet of leaves reduces oxygen levels in the water.

Floating pennywort (*Hydrocotyle ranunculoides*) Bright green shiny leaves with wavy edges, between 5 and 7cm (2–3in) in diameter. It is an extraordinarily fast grower – in the wild, it can grow up to 20cm (8in) a day – and forms very dense mats underwater.

How can I bring my pond to life?

Pondskater

Hydra

Daphnia
(water flea)

YOU THINK YOU'VE DONE EVERYTHING that was recommended setting up your wildlife pond. But you haven't yet seen even a single frog. Is there anything you've overlooked that would bring your pond to life?

Checklist for wildlife

Check that your pond has the must-haves. Is there cover around the pond? Frogs, for instance, don't like trekking across open space because it leaves them vulnerable to predators.

If for any reason you can't plant around your pond margins, a selection of containers planted up with suitable species will work. Is there cover in the pond? Some species don't like too much open water. Can creatures get in and out? If you can't have a shallow 'beach' edge, then a pile of stones or a tilted branch or even a plank of wood tilted into the water will do.

▼ Shallow borders with plenty of cover are an important aspect of any wildlife pond.

How long have you waited?

If you're confident that your pond offers everything it should, you may need to be patient. While it's true that some species arrive at a pond within a day or two, others may take their time, or are dependent on the sort of habitat your garden is close to. Amphibians can take up to a year. Don't forget that not every pond will have all species, so don't fret if you can't tick everything off an 'ideal' list. For example, your pond may become an excellent newt pond, but a neighbour may have a pond full of frogs and toads. Some species are simply more likely than others: many dragonflies favour larger bodies of water, whereas damselflies will show up around even small garden ponds. Pond owners tend to focus on the larger species, sometimes at the cost of becoming familiar with the smaller ones. Pond skaters may not have the immediate appeal of frogs or newts but looked at closely, the habits of your pond's invertebrates can become just as engrossing.

Try a pond dip

Get a good field guide and sweep a net gently through the pond. Empty out the contents into a bucket with an inch or two of pond water in it. Then use a small stick to poke around, gently. You may need a magnifying glass, but you'll soon see that your water is teeming with wildlife already.

If you've set up the habitat, your pond has life already – you just haven't spotted any of the larger or more noticeable species yet. Smaller species, from pond skaters to gnats, often fly in within days, but it can take some of the larger animals longer to arrive.

BACKSWIMMERS AND BOATMEN

It's a rare pond that doesn't have a population of the creatures that used to be grouped together under the name of water boatmen but are now divided into water boatmen and backswimmers. These browny coloured, medium-sized, oval-bodied insects – sometimes with a slightly metallic gleam because of the air bubbles they carry underwater with them – are so familiar that you may never have taken a closer look. Both insects reach around 1.5cm (½in) in length, and both skull around near the surface of almost any body of still water. Look more closely and you'll see that while the lesser water boatman (*Corixa punctata*) swims upright, the common backswimmer (*Notonecta glauca*) does backstroke. They also have different diets: water boatmen are vegetarians, feeding off algae and small plants, but the backswimmer is a successful predator – it will tackle prey as large as a tadpole and can also take insects who have fallen into the water and are held there by surface tension. Movement alerts the backswimmer; it's a fast swimmer and on reaching its prey it speedily administers an incredibly painful, venomous bite. It then sucks out the insides of its incapacitated victim.

Backswimmer   **Water boatman**

Is a water feature as good as a pond?

IF THERE'S A REASON you can't have a wildlife pond, are there any other garden water features that will offer as much to as wide a variety of species? And are any better choices for wildlife than others?

There's a wide choice when it comes to water for wildlife in the garden. Larger basins or fountains will be used by bathing and preening birds (they're best sited separately from feeding stations, and also well away from overhanging bushes or trees, to minimize the danger from predators such as cats). Insects need to drink, too, so even the smallest water offering is useful – set up a bee drinker (see pp109) so that bees can drink safely.

Ponds, even small ones, offer a whole range of water creatures a habitat they can live in or around, either full-time – like pond fleas, water beetles and numerous larvae on the long wait for their final transformation to adults – or as visitors. While water features can't usually offer a full habitat, they can still meet many of the needs of plenty of visiting wildlife, from birds to beetles.

△ Unless that's what you want, a garden water feature doesn't have to be elaborate, although there's evidence that bathing birds particularly enjoy bubbling or falling water.

If you don't have a pond because you have young children and are concerned about safety, you could opt for either a bubble fountain or a bog garden, both of which offer wildlife interest. And if you live somewhere with only hard surfaces, where it's not possible to install a pond, consider a container pond: a wide-topped container can be adapted to appeal to wildlife if you ensure that it has steps or slopes, both inside and out, to allow animals an easy route to climb in and out.

Heat waves

With climate change the weather is getting more unpredictable and extremes of temperature, even in temperate climates, are becoming more common. Heat waves are stressful for wildlife; in a spell of very hot weather, offer as much water as you can in as many spots as possible around the garden. Think laterally, too: if there's extremely dry weather in late March or April, for example, when nest building is at its height, put out a flattish container of wet, pre-mixed mud. When other potential sources have dried up, it will be useful to the species that need mud to construct their nests.

▶ Swallows (*Hirundo rustica*) not only drink and hunt as they skim over open water but also use mud as a key ingredient when constructing their nests.

FROM ORNAMENTAL POOL TO WILDLIFE POND

If you'd like a wildlife pond but you've inherited an ornamental goldfish pond, it's usually possible to convert one into the other. If it's been made with a pond liner and has shallow margins, then all you have to do is to find a new home for the fish and introduce some appropriate planting, both in the pond and around the margins, but even a more formal 'box'-shaped pond with vertical sides can be made wildlife-friendly.

1 If there are fish, relocate them – perhaps with a neighbour or friend with an existing goldfish pond. If there is a pump and filter system, this should be dismantled and removed (and perhaps offered to the new owner of the fish).

2 If the pond has been designed with steep (or even vertical) sides it will need some different levels, and an entrance 'beach' slope constructed to help creatures in and out of the pond. Improvise

with rocks and stones in corners to create 'ladders', or by introducing branches or other pieces of wood. Although it may not be possible to create the shadows that are so desirable, if the water has plenty of plant shelter and easy access, it will still attract wildlife.

3 Check the existing planting and, if necessary, change or augment it with a mix of oxygenating (below the surface) and floating plants, both to offer cover to aquatic wildlife and to keep the oxygen levels in the water up.

▶ Oxygenating plants, such as this pretty water violet (*Hottonia palustris*), not only offer cover for waterlife but also help to maintain the oxygen levels in pond water.

Should I break the ice?

IN A VERY COLD WINTER, your pond may freeze over completely. If it does, should you break the ice to ensure that any wildlife isn't starved of oxygen, or leave well alone?

Dos and don'ts

Research suggests that the wildlife in your pond will cope just fine even if the surface ices over. Ponds freeze from the surface down, and it's not likely that, even in very cold weather, a pond will freeze solid. Also, oxygen diffuses into the pond very slowly – at a rate of 2–3mm (^{1}/10in) per day – which means that any taken in through a de-iced gap will take weeks to reach the bottom of even a 60cm- (25in) deep pond (ponds that are deeper still are more like to suffer from deoxygenation because light can't get into the depths, which strengthens the argument for relatively shallow ones). In very cold weather the wildlife retreats to the lower levels of the pond,

The traditional solution to sheet ice on the pond is to sit a saucepan of hot water on the surface, gradually thawing a hole. In theory, this will ensure that wildlife won't die for lack of oxygen, but really, it's only necessary if your pond is their sole source of drinking water.

so it's unlikely that they'll get any benefit from increased oxygen levels until a particularly cold snap is over.

Received wisdom holds that you shouldn't shatter the ice on a frozen pond if you have fish because it will result in shock waves travelling through the water which will harm them, but as making a hole in the ice does not seem to make much difference in any case, this is a moot point.

There's one thing you can do that will help oxygen levels in the water: if snow has fallen on the iced-over pond, brush it off. Both algae and oxygenating plants will continue to photosynthesize under the ice (although the process will slow in extreme cold), but they won't be able to do so if they don't have any light.

▼ Many species will survive the surface of a pond freezing over, but lying snow should be brushed off – light is necessary for photosynthesis to continue under the ice.

Q Is sun or shade best for a pond?

Many sources tell you that ponds need sun and that the ideal site is one that gets plenty of sunlight. But a lot of natural ponds seem to do quite well in relatively shady settings – so how much of a problem is shade?

Let the light in

If you've inherited a pond that's in partial shade, or your only option for a new pond is relatively shady, do everything you can to open the aspect up and to let as much light in as possible. This may involve cutting back overhanging branches and regularly skimming off fallen leaves from the pond's surface before they sink to the bottom. Don't net shady ponds in order to trap leaves, as netting can catch some larger pond visitors such as frogs and hedgehogs, which won't be able to escape.

Shadier ponds are also best kept shallow as oxygenating plants will only photosynthesize in the light and if oxygen levels in the water are comparatively low, leaf litter in deeper areas is more likely to stagnate. Some fallen leaves in the pond are a healthy part of the habitat, but too many may begin to silt up the pond.

TREES CAN BE GOOD FOR PONDS

Introducing wood to the wildlife pond can benefit a number of species. If you leave a large branch in a corner of your pond, it may become an egg-laying site for a number of dragonfly species, including the brown and southern hawkers. Beetle larvae are likely to move in, feeding either on the rotting wood or on the fungi and algae that colonize it.

Brown hawker,
Aeshna grandis

A sunny site has some natural advantages: the sunlight will keep the oxygenating plants under the water working well, for example. But if you choose your planting carefully, a wildlife pond can usually cope with shade for at least part of the day – and a shadier site will mean you're less likely to have excessive algae.

When should I clear out my pond?

DOES YOUR POND NEED an annual spring clean, or is it better left to its own devices – and if it does need a clear out, what's the best way to tackle it?

Ideally a wildlife pond should mostly be left alone, to offer as natural a habitat as possible to the species who live in it. Some degree of maintenance may sometimes be needed, but it should be carried out carefully to cause the minimum of disruption.

When and why

Let's take the 'why' first. If you see that there's been a really large build-up of sludge, over 20cm (8in), say, at the bottom of the pond – perhaps with too many leaves falling in over a long period – or if the pond water has started to smell stagnant, it's better to remove some mud from the bottom. Plants in mesh containers may have outgrown them or may simply need a haircut, too. When it comes to 'when', spring cleaning is a misnomer for a wildlife pond: if you need to do any clearance, it's best done in late summer, when the water level tends to be at its lowest, pond creatures aren't breeding and amphibians have yet to go into hibernation.

How to do it

Your pond shouldn't be completely emptied: that would mean throwing away all the time you've spent achieving a good balance (not too much algae, clear water and around a third of the surface covered with the leaves of aquatic plants) and a thriving pond life community. If you're taking a proportion of the muddy sludge out at the bottom, do it across two years to minimize the disruption to wildlife. In August/September of the first year, take a few spades of the mud from just one side of the bottom of the pond, going slowly to give any wildlife the chance to shift to the other side as you work and taking care not to puncture

If a pond's surface is covered with heavy leaf fall, scoop some out every day or two to avoid too many sinking into the mud at the bottom of the pond.

SEASONS IN THE POND

Even if you maintain a low-intervention approach, wildlife ponds may still need occasional help. Season by season, here's what's happening:

Spring

If your pond's planting is looking a little thin, late spring is a good time to introduce additional plants and split any existing plants that need it. Don't disrupt amphibian mating time. If you spot frogs mating, leave it a few days before doing any planting work. Add algae control such as barley straw pads.

Summer

Water levels may sink; most wildlife will adjust to this. If there's a heatwave and levels get very low, top the level up a little using rainwater from a water butt. Keep on top of vigorous pond plants by pulling them out as necessary.

Autumn

If leaf fall is heavy or a large quantity of leaves are blowing into the pond, skim some off the surface of the pond with a net or rake. Remove any foliage that is dying back on water lilies or marginals standing in the water.

Winter

The quiet season. Continue to remove leaves from the water surface as necessary. Check wildlife ramps. Leave dead foliage and seedheads on marginal plants if they're clear of the water, as they often provide overwinter shelter for insect species.

the liner (a plastic shovel is best). The following year repeat the exercise, but this time take mud out of the opposite side. To avoid another build-up of mud, extract fallen leaves from the pond every few days in the autumn; when too many sink to the bottom, they gradually rot down to add to the nutrient-rich layer of sludge.

Plants that have become too abundant and are crowding out the pond can be taken out of the water if they are growing in mesh containers, then trimmed or divided to take them back down to their ideal size. Those that are growing without containers can be trimmed by hand to reduce their spread. Leave any clumps of redundant vegetation alongside the pond for a day to allow any wildlife to escape back into the water, then put it on your compost heap.

What is a rain garden?

WHAT'S THE DIFFERENCE between a rain garden and a bog or marsh garden – and how can you make and maintain one?

How rain gardens work

Rain gardens first became popular in the US in the 1990s, but over the last two decades their appeal has spread much further afield and they're appearing more often, both in private gardens and in public areas, in Europe and the UK. They are quite different from bog- or marsh gardens because rather than being perpetually soggy like the latter, they're sporadically waterlogged when there's heavy rain, then drain slowly but completely, returning the rainwater into the ground or allowing it to be taken up by strategic planting. The undesirable alternative (unless you have enough water butts to take every drop of rainfall) would be to allow rain to run off impermeable surfaces and go straight into storm drains. Particularly in urban or suburban environments, rain gardens are used to help alleviate the flood risk that heavy rain increasingly presents because so many areas that were previously gardens or other green spaces have been built on or paved over.

Wildlife pluses

As well as being generally good for the environment, a rain garden can, depending on the plants chosen for it, offer an additional patch of pollinator-friendly flowers, food plants for caterpillars or benefits for birds in the shape of berry-bearing shrubs.

How to make a rain garden

The rain garden needs to be a saucer shape, with extremely shallow sloping sides, a flat base (sometimes lined with gravel to assist drainage) and a bank around the edges to ensure the water is contained and can't run off. This bank, or berm, can be made from compacted soil, or a rain garden can be sited within a space that's otherwise paved, with the water directed into a cleared, recessed area of soil that's been planted up.

A rain garden is a shallow depression which has been created to take advantage of water run-off from the roof(s) of an adjacent building or buildings. In the average plot, a rain garden will be fairly small; as a rule of thumb, it should be about one-fifth the size of the roof which supplies it with water.

Rain gardens should be sited at least 3m (10ft) from house walls or other buildings, and the rain should be channelled directly into them, whether by means of an extension pipe or a narrow dug-out channel or rill. You can even make a storm-water planter, feeding run-off directly from a downpipe into a trough or planter filled with wet-tolerant plants, and installing an overflow pipe at one side.

GOOD PLANTS FOR RAIN GARDENS

By their very nature, rain gardens are most suitable for plants that can tolerate being waterlogged for short periods, then slowly drained. There's a wide range of options; here is just a handful of possibilities.

Dogwood (*Cornus sanguinea*) A handsome shrub (right) with bright red stems and winter berries for the birds. Its leaves are food plants for some species of case-bearer moth.

Inula (*Inula hookeri*) A hairy-stemmed perennial with vivid yellow daisy-like flowers in later summer and early autumn. It's popular with pollinators and will tolerate some shade.

Sneezeweed (*Helenium* sp.) Attractive clump-forming perennials in a range of colours from bright yellows (below) through to orange and dark red, good for pollinators.

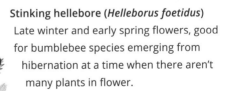

Stinking hellebore (*Helleborus foetidus*) Late winter and early spring flowers, good for bumblebee species emerging from hibernation at a time when there aren't many plants in flower.

Black-eyed Susan (*Rudbeckia hirta*) Orange-yellow flowers with black centres. Very popular with pollinators.

Chapter 4

Hands-on Help

Is a hedgehog out in daylight in trouble?

You know that hedgehogs are nocturnal – so what would one be doing out and about in daylight? Is there a problem, how do you know whether there is or not, and should you intervene?

Hedgehogs don't thrive on interference. Healthy 'hogs are best left alone, so you need to be fairly sure there's a problem before you intervene. If the hedgehog you saw was a nesting female, she'll be alert and busy, and you may even spot a mouthful of straw or leaves. Leave her be.

Hurt hedgehogs

If a hedgehog is out in daylight and isn't moving, is moving sluggishly or is walking in circles, there's a problem, and there's a range of possibilities as to what that might

Healthy hedgehogs aren't usually seen during the day, but a nesting female may be spotted out on summer afternoons or early mornings, collecting bedding material or foraging for food. However, a hedgehog that's out in the daytime at other times of year, or one that isn't lively and active, is probably in trouble.

be. It may be ill or hurt. If it's winter, it may have emerged from hibernation too early, perhaps because it was disturbed, and be too weak or hungry to manage for itself. Or it may have been attacked by another animal. Sometimes you'll find a hedgehog caught in netting or wire – if so, clip it out, but leave any detailed untangling to a specialist or a vet.

What to do

If the hedgehog looks inert, look up a number for your local wildlife centre and call for advice before you take action – they'll be able to give on-the-spot guidance. If you can't get hold of a wildlife centre, call a vet.

Whether or not there are any obvious wounds, pick it up gently (use thick gardening gloves): a hedgehog that doesn't curl up when picked up is a sick hedgehog, but even if it does curl up, it may still need help. Offer a dish of water – it may be dehydrated – but don't feed it.

Ideally, it needs to see a specialist as quickly as possible. To transport a hedgehog, you need a pair of gloves, a deep cardboard box or pet carrier, a pile of soft towels or cloth and a hot water bottle filled with hot (not boiling) water. Line the box with towels, with the hot water bottle wrapped in towels at the bottom, pick the hedgehog up with gloves, put it in the box, handling it as deftly as possible, close the box, making sure there's enough air getting in and get going. Don't try to 'reassure' the hedgehog, handle it as little as possible; like all wild animals, it will find human contact stressful. Gloves are important, not just because of the prickles, but because hedgehogs can carry ringworm or salmonella, both of which are transferrable to humans. (Don't worry about fleas, though – hedgehog fleas are hedgehog-only.)

HIBERNATING HEDGEHOGS

A healthily hibernating hedgehog will have put enough weight on to survive the winter before going into its nest in October or November. If you accidentally disturb one, cover it back up as quickly as possible, leave a saucer of moist cat food nearby in case you've roused it enough for it to need to replenish its supplies and give the site and its immediate surroundings as wide a berth as possible till spring. Research has shown that it's actually not uncommon for hedgehogs to wake and move hibernation sites once or twice in the course of the winter, so, having been disturbed, don't worry if it decides to relocate.

▶ Hedgehogs often move sites mid-hibernation, so disturbing one isn't disastrous provided that there's plenty of shelter (and ideally a square meal) nearby.

I disturbed a bird's nest: will it be OK?

Trimming the hedge in mid-spring, you found a thrush's nest with some eggs in it. There wasn't a bird sitting on them. Will the parent bird abandon it, and what's the best thing for you to do? Should you just leave it where it is?

Early days

If the thrush wasn't already sitting on the nest, it may be that she hadn't finished laying her clutch of eggs yet. Lots of bird species lay their clutch with gaps between the eggs and only start to incubate when they've laid the last egg (this means that the eggs will hatch more or less simultaneously). Chances are that, if this is the case and the shelter around the nest hasn't been too drastically compromised,

the bird will return, lay the last egg or two, and then incubate the clutch as usual. If the nesting pair were disturbed enough to decide to abandon the nest, at least it's early enough in the season for them to make a fresh start elsewhere and have the chance of raising another brood successfully.

The risk factor

Studies show that most birds, when disturbed nesting, take the degree of disturbance into account. If it is so great that there seems no prospect of raising their young successfully, and it is early enough in the season to make a fresh start with a new nest and eggs, they will abandon the existing nest and start again in a new site, but when there's only a slight disturbance, they'll often stay put.

What you can take away from the experience is that any major cutting back or tidying needs to be done

◀ Treat likely sites such as shrubs, hedges and dense climbers with respect during nesting season; if you accidentally find a nest, leave it alone and don't hover around nearby.

ARE NESTS REUSED?

Given the amount of work that goes into making a nest, you might think that their creators would want to get the maximum use out of them. But some species, even those that raise several broods in a year, will usually make a new nest for each new clutch of eggs (although rather than starting from scratch, they tend to recycle, partially dismantling the old nest and using its components for the new version). Although it makes more work, it ensures that the possibility of a nest harbouring unwelcome parasites or infections is kept to a minimum. Migrants, while often returning to the same nesting site year after year, will often build a new nest, although some, such as house martins, will consider a fixer-upper, which they will re-plaster with fresh coats of mud.

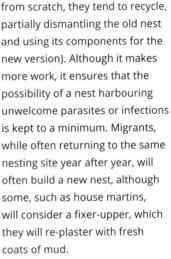
House martins (*Delichon urbicum*) often return to the same nesting sites in successive years but will build a new nest – or at least refurbish the old one – each time.

outside the breeding season. In a number of countries, including the UK, it's illegal to knowingly disrupt nesting birds (and of course if you do it by accident, it's upsetting in any case). Follow the farming model, which ensures that hedge-cutting and non-essential tree surgery doesn't happen between the beginning of March and the end of August, leaving birds free to build their nests and raise their young undisturbed.

A It depends on the extent of the disturbance. If you trimmed nearby but the nest isn't fully exposed, stop work, tuck a cut stem or two over any small gaps in cover you may have left, and leave things alone. As to whether or not the parent birds will return, it's still likely if the nest is now left alone.

A bumblebee stung me: will it die?

YOU WERE FIXING A CLEMATIS back to the wall and accidentally disturbed a feeding bumblebee which was alarmed enough to sting you. The sting hurt, but you've put antihistamine on it. What will the consequences be for the bee?

How bee stings work

Only wasp or bee females can sting (the sting is a modified oviposter, or egg-laying organ, so is exclusive to females), and the sting itself consists of a stylus (the 'needle') which is held between two lancets that are used to push and pull the needle as the venom of the sting is delivered from the venom sac. In honeybees, the lancets have pronounced barbs and become so deeply embedded that the bee can't usually pull them out without taking a proportion of its undercarriage with them, which is why a honeybee will probably die if it stings you. But in social wasps and bumblebees the lancets have comparatively tiny barbs which, while they hold your skin efficiently enough for the venom to be delivered, are more easily withdrawn, and so the insect will usually survive the sting.

HOW AN EGG-LAYING ORGAN TURNED INTO A STING

There's a long evolutionary history attached, but the ovipositor originally developed with the capacity to lay eggs into things (for example, in parasitoid species, the ovipositor has to break the skin of the host species to lay its eggs). This meant that it developed a capacity to pierce, and over time, in some species, its function became to defend instead of, or in some cases as well as, to reproduce.

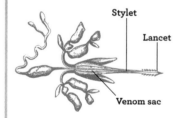

Stylet
Lancet
Venom sac

Contrary to popular belief, a bumblebee won't usually die if it uses its sting. Nor will a common wasp, or most of the many other species of bees and wasps that have a sting. A honeybee, on the other hand, will usually die if it uses its sting.

My bird feeders are attracting rats: should I put poison out?

EVEN THE KEENEST wildlife enthusiast has a limit, and that may be reached when rats turn up in your garden. There's actually much to admire about rats – they are social, smart and interesting – but they harbour a range of diseases, and when it comes to tunnels in the garden, they will try the patience of the most tolerant gardener.

Short rations

If rats are enjoying your garden, it's because you are unwittingly supplying them with food and shelter. Reduce the hospitality, and they will move on to somewhere more welcoming. The food aspect is straightforward to deal with. Ideally you should suspend feeding the birds for a time, but if you don't want to, put out only small amounts of food on raised tables and feeders (not scattered on the ground), use no-mess mixes to reduce spilt food and clear any that remains at the end of each day, so none is left overnight: rats are mostly nocturnal. Move the feeders around to different spots in your garden, too, so that rats can't just go to the same place for a daily feed.

Don't add any potential foodstuffs to your compost heap for a while; limit additions to twigs and grass clippings, and take the opportunity to give your compost a thorough turn. Move any other supplies

If you've spotted rats around your bird feeders there is plenty of action you can take to make your garden less appealing to them. Poison should definitely be avoided; not only is it inhumane, but there's a risk that you may poison not only the rats, but also predators of rats, such as owls, by introducing poison into the food chain.

that might have rat appeal, bins of pet food, for example, into the house.

If you know where the rats are coming into the garden, small holes can be blocked up. Rat runs and burrows can also be made inhospitable with balls of chicken wire placed in burrow entrances. If you have a cat, used cat litter can be effective if it's tipped into the burrows, too.

Can I revive a distressed bee?

YOU'VE FOUND A LARGE BUMBLEBEE lying on a paving stone. It looks dead, but when you gently pick it up, it moves very slightly. What's wrong, and what's the best way to help it out?

In autumn

If you find an exhausted bumblebee at the end of summer or in early autumn, have a look at its wings. By this time of the year, they'll likely show wear and tear, with slightly ragged edges: a bumblebee will have been flying and foraging since spring and is reaching the end of its life. As bumblebee species have been recorded spending 7.5 hours a day collecting and carrying food, including up to 16 return visits to their home colony each day, it's perhaps no surprise that it looks a little worse for wear. If there's an open flower nearby, put the bumblebee alongside it to give it a chance to feed if it's able, but otherwise don't intervene.

SUGAR SNACKS

Why refined white sugar? Wouldn't brown sugar or even watered-down honey be better for a bee? No; brown sugar has additional solids in it from the molasses it's distilled from, and honey can carry bee diseases. Plain white sugar solution is best. Don't think, either, that because you revived a bee, it's a good idea to leave out saucers of sugar solution to help out any tired passing bee. Sugar solution may attract bees, but it will distract them from their day job: collecting nectar (which contains other ingredients such as amino-acids, that are beneficial to bees) and gathering pollen. Making sure your garden is planted up with plenty of nectar- and pollen-rich flowers is a better long-term strategy.

▶ A bee's natural diet is found in nectar- and pollen-rich plants such as this common heather (*Calluna vulgaris*) – sugar is only a quick energy fix.

That depends on what season it is. If it's autumn, it's likely that the bee has reached the end of its life and there won't be much you can do for it. If it's late winter or early spring, though, it's a different story: you've probably found a bumblebee queen, and you should be able to help her. Bumblebees can also get bedraggled after a heavy summer downpour.

A metal beer bottle lid is the perfect serving dish for your sugared water solution.

In spring

An exhausted bumblebee in early spring is probably a young queen who has emerged early from hibernation but hasn't managed to collect enough food to maintain the energy to fly. This is the time of year when she needs to be out looking for a nesting site to enable her to establish a colony. If there are open flowers she can be helped on to, their nectar are the best boost; however, if it's still very early in the season and there aren't many flowers out, you can feed and warm her up to enable her to continue her work.

Bee boost

Pick her up gently with a glove or on any surface you can carry her on – she's highly unlikely to sting you. Mix up a solution of one-third processed white sugar to two-thirds water. Once the sugar has dissolved, pour a tiny quantity of the mixture into a bottle cap (it needs to be a very small, shallow container with a flat rim, so that the bee can both reach the liquid and avoid getting it on her fur or wings, which will make them sticky and compromise her flying ability). Put the bee alongside the bottle cap; a hungry bee that's otherwise healthy will quickly extend her proboscis and drink. Give her enough time to finish drinking then, if the weather isn't too bad, carry her back outside and leave her in a sheltered spot so she can fly off. If it's almost night-time or the weather is terrible, put her gently into a plastic box with a few leaves and anchor a paper towel over the top, so there's plenty of air but she's confined, then release her the following morning. Don't keep her longer than you have to: she needs to find a nesting site, and she can't do that in your kitchen, even if you're keeping her safe.

Placed near a sugary liquid, an exhausted bumblebee won't usually need nudging: she'll quickly locate it, extend her proboscis and start drinking.

What should I do with a winter butterfly?

I've found a peacock butterfly fluttering around indoors – and it's midwinter. Can I help it to survive until spring, and if so, how?

Peacock butterfly
Aglais io

The peacock is often one of the first butterflies you spot in spring; if the weather is warm enough, you may see it out and about in March.

Peacocks (*Aglais io*) are one of the butterfly species that may enter a state, specific to insects, called diapause, in order to get through the winter months. Diapause is similar to hibernation, but the butterfly will need cool conditions for it to be successful. It won't survive in a heated interior, so it should be taken somewhere cooler.

This isn't because it has an exceptionally speedy breeding programme: these early butterflies overwintered as adults.

What is diapause?

Diapause is unlike hibernation as only homeothermic (warm-blooded) animals lower their metabolism to enter hibernation. An insect may enter it as a larva, a pupa or an adult but won't grow or develop while in diapause, instead existing in a state of suspended animation. Insects will look for shelter in a quiet corner as temperatures drop and day length shortens. Some butterfly and ladybird species will seek shelter in buildings

---

BEATING THE FREEZE

The formation of ice crystals causes damage to living cells, but some insects have a particularly useful biochemical trick when the temperatures drop: in a cold snap, they produce quantities of glycerol, which enables their bodies to cool to very low temperatures without actually freezing: a sort of inbuilt antifreeze. When the weather warms up again, the glycerol levels in their systems go back down.

over the winter, but they still need their surroundings to be cool; what has happened with this peacock is that the warmth of the central heating has woken it and disrupted its over-wintering pattern.

What you should do

The butterfly is awake, but there aren't flowers for it to feed on, and if it's left in a too-warm room, it will use up its energy reserves and die. To save it, catch it (gently) and confine it in a medium-sized cardboard box with slits or air holes, so there's plenty of air but it can't escape. Once boxed, put it somewhere cool (perhaps a shelf in the fridge, or an outdoor porch). After a couple of hours when it has quietened down, move the box somewhere dark and cool – a garage or shed, perhaps – where it can safely wait out the winter. It should stay in the box; if you let it out while it's still awake, it's likely to head straight for a window where there are often spiders and cobwebs. Don't forget it, though; when warmer weather arrives, carefully open a crack in the lid and the garage or shed window so it can leave when it's ready.

WINTER GETAWAYS

Some insects simply leave cold weather behind them altogether: insect migration is a huge subject that is only just beginning to be understood. A study made in 2009 established that painted lady butterflies (weighing under a gram each) make an annual migration of an almost unbelievable 14,500km (9,000 miles), arriving in Northern Europe and the UK in summer, and returning to Africa in winter. The journey may occupy several generations of the butterfly (they breed at spots along the way, and the new generation takes on the next leg of the journey), but they're not often spotted on land because they make large parts of the flight at an altitude of 900m (3,000ft), flying at a maximum speed of almost 50kmph (30mph).

▶ The delicate appearance of the painted lady butterfly (*Vanessa cardui*) belies the stamina that's called for in the course of its extraordinary migratory journey.

Q Should I move a lone fledgling?

THERE'S A BABY BLACKBIRD sitting on the grass. It has plenty of downy feathers but it evidently can't fly yet. Has it been abandoned?

Although it's quite widely believed that fledglings can fly straight from the nest, this is only true of a very few species, including swifts. Most fledglings spend a few days on the ground while their feathers mature enough for them to fly properly. In the meantime, they can hop, practice with short, fluttering flights and sometimes also run surprisingly fast. Their parents usually have several fledglings scattered about, and they will return and care for them in turn up to the point at which they're able to fly properly – and sometimes beyond it. Once fledged, birds don't usually return to the nest.

▼ A fluffy but fully-feathered fledgling may actually be safer in a quiet corner of the garden than in a nest that it and its siblings have outgrown.

A Most birds leave the nest before they can fly properly and spend a few days on the ground. Even though you can't see the parents, they're almost certainly in the vicinity. It's best left alone unless it's in immediate danger.

Nest may not be best

Why are young birds leaving, or being pushed out of, the nest when they're not equipped to cope? As they grow larger, the nest is probably less safe than the outside world. A nestful of baby birds is both noisy – with the competitive cheeping of the young for food – and smelly which, together with the parents' regular visits, make it easier for predators, such as magpies, cats or squirrels, to spot. And if a predator finds the nest, none of the brood will survive. Outside the nest, the fledglings are scattered, so one predator is unlikely to take the lot, and while they may not be highly mobile, they can still move around a fair amount, making them less of a sitting target.

The outside world

Nevertheless, the world is a dangerous place for new fledglings, and they do succumb either to predators or hunger in quite large numbers. Parent birds will feed them and teach them to manage for themselves for a couple of weeks but will eventually move on, often starting to rear another brood before the end of the summer.

Although it may seem brutal, many garden birds' broods are big enough to cope with quite dramatic losses. Blue tits can raise up to 13 chicks from a single clutch of eggs, and even the more moderate blackbird, with between 3 and 5 chicks per clutch, may produce as many as four separate broods over a good summer. Realistically, it's best to shoo away any cats or magpies you see hovering (and confine your own cat indoors when there are fledglings about) and keep your fingers crossed that this fledgling will be one of the (many) lucky ones.

THE THREE AGES OF BABY BIRDS

Hatchling

Recently hatched, it has naked skin with just a few wisps of downy feather developing. Its eyes are closed and it is helpless outside the nest. If you find one on the ground that is still alive and you can see the nest, it's fine to put it back. It's a myth that parent birds will 'smell' you on their baby and reject it: usually, birds will readily accept a baby bird returned to the nest.

Nestling

It's between three days and two weeks old, its eyes are open, it's downy with feathers breaking through the skin (you can see the white, tube-like quills), it's unable to fly and isn't ready to leave the nest yet. As with a hatchling, if you find one on the ground and it's possible to return it to the nest, you should.

Fledgling

It's two weeks or older, well covered in feathers and with a short tail. It can hop, perch and flutter. At this stage, once it's left the nest, it is unlikely to return, and shouldn't be put back there. Its parents will care for it on the ground until it's fully able to fly.

▶ A hatchling needs its parents and won't survive away from the nest.

Q Can you relocate a bumblebee nest?

BUMBLEBEES HAVE BUILT a nest quite near your house. Is it going to cause a problem when you're going in and out and, if so, is it possible to move it?

B umblebees are less likely to sting you than honeybees but, like most other species, may move to defend their nest if they feel under threat. Bumblebee colonies live for a matter of two or three months, so it's best to see if you can arrange things to let the bees take care of their business without interruption.

Bumblebees usually choose sites that are both sheltered and out of the way for their nests. Depending on the species, you may find one in the base of a hedge, occupying an abandoned mouse's nest or in an old bird box. However, occasionally one will encroach on human living space. When that happens, it's better to work around the nest than to try to move it.

▼ There's no guarantee that shifting a disrupted bumblebee nest will be successful – if at all possible, it's better to try to leave it alone until it vacates naturally in late summer.

Good neighbours

First, how close to the nest do people really have to walk? If the answer is 'not very', then post a notice near the nest so that people know to give it a wide berth.

What about if bumblebees are actually nesting in your house, under the eaves, or in the loft space? In that case, be aware that bumblebees don't do structural damage, and a bumblebee nest is a short-term tenancy, lasting at its longest three months.

Create a back door

If a nest is making things really difficult, bumblebee specialists advise that redirecting the bees' entrance route is more likely to be successful than trying to relocate the nest; the latter isn't recommended unless you can get professional help from, say, your local beekeeping society. For example, bees have made a nest on the inside roof of your porch, so they need to fly past people's heads to get out to forage. If you can run a pipe to reroute the nest's existing entrance, instead taking it out of the side of the porch, you'll have solved the problem. A piece of tubing such as a hosepipe or a rigid pipe will do, but it should have a diameter of at least 2cm (1in) and it must be arranged to run slightly downwards, so water can't run into the nest. Install it after dark, when the bees will all be in the nest. Simply pre-mix some soil and water into a thick mud, like plaster, then align one end of the pipe with the existing entrance and

QUEEN'S SLEEP DISTURBED

In winter, when old bumblebee colonies are dead and the new ones aren't yet established, gardeners may accidentally disturb a solo hibernating bumblebee queen. If you're doing some winter clearance and find one (they usually hibernate in small burrows in the soil, or you'll occasionally encounter them in plant pots), cover her back up with soil, leaves or whatever was protecting her. Pack it loosely; she needs to be able to dig her way out easily when she wakes up.

If she has woken up (if she's buzzing audibly, she's definitely awake) and there aren't any nectar plants out yet for her to feed from, leave a small lid of sugar water (see pp145) nearby to give her the opportunity to feed.

arrange the other where you want the bees to exit and entrance, and use the mud to fix the pipe in place. Watch the next day to ensure that the pipe connection is clear and that bees are flying in and out of the new entrance.

Why are my frogs dying?

YOU WERE SHOCKED TO FIND several frogs floating dead in your pond. What caused it, and could you have prevented it?

What happened?

You weren't responsible for the death of the pond's frogs, nor could you really have done anything to prevent it. In instances of winterkill, it's believed that frogs are killed either by anoxia – a lack of available oxygen in the water – or by the release of toxic gases that are produced by the natural decomposition of dead plant material that has accumulated in the bottom of the pond, or a mixture of both. Occasionally, in prolonged sub-zero temperatures, shallow ponds will freeze either completely or partially, which will kill frogs. While a frozen pond isn't necessarily immediately short of oxygen, the frogs that do overwinter in the water (many opt to find shelter on land instead) tend to go to the deepest areas where oxygen is naturally in shorter supply, breathing through their skin. Even if a pond isn't frozen over completely, oxygen from the surface takes a long time to make its way down to the depths, and although oxygenating plants and algae will continue to work in low temperatures and light levels, production slows down. (If there's ice covered by a layer of snow on the pond, the resulting darkness will stop them altogether, so always sweep snow off the surface of a frozen pond.)

Ranavirus and its effects

At other times of the year, dead frogs are more likely to have been the victims of ranavirus. This is a particularly nasty disease which can cause skin ulcers and internal bleeding in amphibians: sometimes symptoms

---

LONG LIVE AMPHIBIANS

Amphibians are among the longer-lived inhabitants of the garden – newts live for an average of six years, frogs usually make it up to eight years and toads have the greatest longevity of all, clocking up as many as 12 years.

European common frog, *Rana temporaria*

A What happened to the frogs may depend on what season it is. If it's winter or early spring and your pond has recently been frozen, the mortalities are probably the result of a natural phenomenon called winterkill; if it's later in the spring or summer, the likeliest culprit is a disease called ranavirus.

are visible, at other times the afflicted frog won't display symptoms, although it may look very thin. Ranavirus is found all over the world. It arrived in the UK in the 1980s and its actions and effects aren't yet completely understood, but it can kill frogs singly or infect large groups. Once it's arrived in a population, small or large, ranavirus invariably reduces numbers and in extreme cases can wipe them out altogether. On a more positive note, in recent years scientists have speculated that some frogs seem to have immunity and this may increase over time, leading populations to recover. Ranavirus is the principal

reason that it's important not to move amphibians or their spawn between ponds or other areas of water – you don't want unwittingly to spread it to a healthy population. With either ranavirus or winterkill deaths, it's best to bury the frogs as quickly as possible. And if you suspect ranavirus, wash your gloves and footwear thoroughly before using them again.

In the UK, you can go online and submit a report of amphibian deaths at gardenwildlifehealth.org – this will help to build an understanding of the state of amphibian health across the country.

Breeding younger

Although ranavirus is a rather gloomy topic, there's some evidence that frogs may be developing to cope with the disease and its effects. It's been found that frogs from populations in which ranavirus is present breed younger – at around two years old – than in those where it isn't, in which the usual breeding age is closer to four years old.

▶ Ranavirus doesn't always leave visible signs on an affected frog, although if you find one with visible ulcers or lesions on its skin, it's likely to be suffering from the disease.

Is there anything I can do about molehills?

It's spring and molehills are appearing in your garden. While you've no gripe with moles in principle, the mess is a nuisance and you've twisted your ankle in one of the shallow tunnels. Is there any humane way to get rid of the mole?

Moles (*Talpa europaea*) are some of the most rarely seen visitors to the garden – they spend their lives underground, meeting other moles only to mate. The tunnel system that's disrupting your garden is seasonal, so the most realistic approach for the wildlife gardener is to manage the disruption for a few months each year.

Life underground

Moles dig two kinds of tunnels: permanent ones, built deep underground, which may be used by several generations, and semi-permanent ones, close to the surface, which are used to access food. Their food consists of earthworms and the insects and larvae found in the soil.

Although they're alleged to dislike numerous things, from citronella and ultrasonic devices to the vibrations through the soil caused by someone jumping up and down, none has really been proven to work. Even 'live' traps aren't recommended: the trapped mole will often die of shock before it can be retrieved from the soil.

What to do?

Regularly shovel up the soil from molehills if they're on a lawn area to stop them killing the grass. But you can wait until new surface tunnels have ceased to appear before repairing them: moles only throw up molehills when they first move into a territory. To flatten out tunnels that are close to the surface, dampen the area over and around them then roll the area directly over them with a heavy garden roller. Collapsed surface tunnels need filling in on a lawn to maintain an even surface.

◀ There's one consolation for the gardener 'suffering' from mole damage: the fine tilth thrown up by a digging mole to make molehills makes an all-round excellent potting medium.

How should I handle an injured bird?

THERE'S A SMALL BIRD in the garden that's dragging a wing; it seems alert but it clearly can't fly. Should you try to get it to help and if so, how can you pick it up without hurting it?

Assess from a distance

Make a realistic assessment before trying to catch the bird. Even a bad injury to, say, its leg, may not stop it flying away, and if you can't catch it, you don't want to cause it additional stress. If you're doubtful about being able to catch it, it may be best to leave nature to take its course. If you think you can catch it, be as quick and calm as possible.

Putting your hand gently over a smaller bird's back, with its head protruding from between your fingers, is the safest way to pick it up when it's injured.

Catch and contain

Shut pets inside. Get a cardboard box or other container ready, lined with a towel and with a lid or towel to fold over the top, before you catch the bird. Keeping it still and dark will help avoid aggravating shock. A small bird, up to the size of a thrush or a blackbird, can be held in one hand. Lay your hand over its back, so its head emerges between your fourth and middle finger, so that it's held still with its wings against its body. A slightly larger bird, such as a pigeon, can be held in both hands, a hand over each wing. Wear gloves if possible; if it isn't possible, wash your hands as soon as you can after handling the bird.

An injured bird should see a vet or wildlife specialist as soon as possible. The most helpful thing you can do is to get it into a secure, ventilated, dark container quickly, causing as little stress as you can, then take it to a wildlife centre.

Get to help

Once the bird is in the box, call the number of a vet or local wildlife centre to give them advance warning that you're bringing a bird in to them.

Q I have late-autumn tadpoles; can I save them?

IT'S WELL INTO AUTUMN, but you spotted some tadpoles in your pond, and they don't even have rudimentary legs yet. Why haven't they turned into frogs, and is there anything you can do to speed up their metamorphosis before winter comes?

A It's too late in the season for these tadpoles to change, so they'll overwinter in the pond in their tadpole state and survivors will turn into frogs in the spring when warmer weather comes.

Frogspawn, hatches 2–4 weeks after being laid

Hatchling tadpole with external gills

Lungs develop, skin covers gills

Front legs develop

There's a whole raft of reasons why tadpoles may not turn into frogs on the usual timetable – the usual timetable is spawn laid in the spring, hatching into tadpoles at around three weeks, leaving the pond and then transforming into frogs by around 16 weeks. Overcrowding, a shortage of food or a cold spring and summer, resulting in the pond's water remaining chilly, may all result in a slowdown in the tadpoles' development. Tadpoles eat voraciously until they reach a good weight, then a sudden rise in their production of leptin, a hormone which can suppress appetite, prompts numerous body changes. They stop eating while the long gut of the tadpole herbivore

 The metamorphosis of a tadpole into a tiny frog takes about 16 weeks (stages may take more or less time depending on the temperature and living conditions), although frogs usually then take about three years to reach sexual maturity.

transforms into the short one of the carnivorous frog; the cartilage that made up the tadpole's skull gradually changes to bone and takes on the characteristic broad 'frog' shape, and the gills disappear as the new froglet's lungs start to work. When all four legs are developed and the tail has disappeared, the tadpole has become a frog.

Autumn tadpoles are a natural phenomenon, and it's not necessary to worry about their well-being. For whichever reason, once summer is over their metamorphosis is delayed until the following spring. In the meantime, they will hunker down in the pond, and although they may become less active as the weather chills, they will usually continue to eat. This means that if they survive till spring, they will be a good weight and their chances of completing the transformation into sturdy frogs are high.

Forever young

In a tiny number of cases, tadpoles will never develop into frogs, but will remain stuck in the earlier life stage until they die. This is because they've been born lacking a gene which produces the hormone thyroxine, usually produced in the thyroid gland and, along with leptin, is one of the hormones essential for growth. They may last for several seasons, but they will never metamorphose.

Hind legs develop

Tail shortens

Adult frog

CAN YOU MOVE FROGSPAWN FROM A PUDDLE?

Occasionally frogspawn is spotted in a site that seems completely unsuitable – a shallow rain puddle, for example – where it won't have a chance of hatching and developing without drying out. The reasons for this aren't completely understood, although frogs have a strong instinct to return to places where they themselves were spawned, so it's possible that the puddle was the nearest water to a missing or filled-in pond. Because of the risk of accidentally spreading disease or (when moving the water surrounding the spawn) invasive or unwanted aquatic plants, experts usually recommend that you don't move frogspawn, but when in such shallow water it's not likely that you'll bring much with it. If, left to itself, it will certainly dry out, put it in a bucket and either find a pond it can be moved to (with the permission of the owner) or take it as an opportunity to build a small pond of your own.

Should I let ladybirds overwinter in the house?

LADYBIRDS HAVE A LONG FAST over the winter. Like some other insects, they enter a resting state called diapause which can last from autumn until spring. If you find a group of them in the house – and it does tend to be a group – should you let them stay, or is it better to encourage them to take up winter quarters somewhere else?

△ In summer and autumn, ladybirds tend to lead solitary lives, but they group together over winter – when one finds a good shelter, it releases pheromones which bring others to join it.

Ladybirds indoors

When they make their way indoors – often through the tiniest gaps in the corners of windows or doors – ladybirds tend to cluster together in ceiling corners or behind curtains. To move them, usher them gently into a shoebox (a soft brush works well), then position the whole box in a cooler garage, outhouse or alongside a sheltered log pile if you have one (they like sheltering under the bark), leaving the lid of the box partially off, so they can escape when they want to.

Which ladybird?

There are 46 species of ladybird native to the UK; across Europe, the count goes up to around 250. But you won't find many of them indoors. The 2-spot (*Adalia bipunctata*), 7-spot (*Coccinella septempunctata*) and, over and above all the rest, the harlequin ladybird (*Harmonia axyridis*), a non-native newcomer to the UK and many parts

of Europe, are the species you're most likely to find inside. Not all ladybirds are the classic red-with-black-spots that most of us are familiar with from our earliest storybooks. The different species are also notoriously hard to identify for the non-specialist, even with the most detailed field guide to hand.

Overwintering insects need to remain cool in order to stay in diapause. In warm surroundings they will wake, and any activity will use up the energy stores they have for the winter; in the absence of fresh available food, this may cause them to starve. So, the answer is to collect them up and put them in a cooler place so they remain dormant.

INVASION OF THE HARLEQUINS

It sounds like a science fiction film; over the last fifteen years or so, news of a harlequin ladybird 'plague' has featured heavily in the press. This species was originally a native of Asia; having been introduced around the world as a biological control, it has gradually spread. In both Europe and the UK it's been accused of squeezing out some of the native species – it is thought that the harlequins may be out-competing natives for food. They may also help spread diseases and pathogens for which natives have no immunity, out-competing them for food and shelter, and even eating the larvae and eggs of other ladybirds. From the spotter's viewpoint, it's tricky to identify; it has over 30 different possible 'liveries', although in the UK it's the only species which has orange legs, and whose lavae is spikey and has two distinctive orange stripes, while the larvae of most native species are black or grey. Specialists believe that the original grim prognosis – that it would decimate native ladybird species – will probably not come to pass; there's evidence that native predators, including some species of parasitic wasp, have already begun to prey on the newcomers.

A ladybird life cycle

Adult ladybirds usually emerge from diapause in March and by May are ready to mate. They lay their yellow eggs in clusters on leaves, usually close to the aphids which will be their larvae's main food supply. The tiny larvae hatch out within 10 days, then start to feed and grow energetically, moulting four times before pupating between four and six weeks later. The pupal stage lasts for around a fortnight, then the adult emerges. It's a plain yellow colour at first; the darker colour and the spots appear after a few hours as the body shell hardens.

▼ Life cycle of the two-spot ladybird (*Adalia bipunctata*). Left to right: eggs grouped on underside of leaf; young larva covered in white wax; full-grown larva; pupa attached to leaf; the adult beetle.

Should I appreciate a sparrowhawk in my garden?

IT'S A SHARP REMINDER of the red-in-tooth-and-claw element in nature: garden birds were gathered at your outdoor feeder when a sparrowhawk swooped down, collected a blue tit and proceeded to dine. Can you – and should you – do anything to stop it happening again?

Top predator

In principle you know that if the sparrowhawk hadn't swooped on the blue tit in your garden, it would have been eating another bird or animal somewhere else. Even if in practice it's hard to accept, enjoy the fact that such a high-level predator visited; it's a sign that there are enough small birds and animals to keep the next stage up the food chain fed. Sparrowhawks are extraordinarily beautiful, and the chance to see one close up shouldn't be dismissed. In the 1950s, the chances of seeing one would have been extremely remote, as the sparrowhawk population in the UK and many parts of Europe had been decimated by the use of organochlorine pesticides – now banned – and the breed was highly endangered.

Sparrowhawk,
Accipiter nisus

Do they harm songbird populations?

The evidence shows that sparrowhawks don't affect songbird populations adversely; in fact, they may ultimately strengthen them because hawks will catch those birds that are slower (and pick off old and sick individuals, too). The fastest, fittest birds will escape and go on to breed.

All these factors make the presence of a sparrowhawk in your garden a cause for celebration, but if you'd prefer the smaller birds to feed undisturbed, you need to look at possible deterrents.

Things hawks don't like

Users report mixed results from some popular options, but they're worth a try. You can hang CDs or reflective strips in a protective screen around your feeders, which will restrict the sparrowhawk's ability to dive, although you'll need to judge the distance they hang from the feeders carefully, so that they don't also put off the smaller birds you're trying to protect. 'Seeing eye' balloons are available to buy. They mimic an immense eyeball, complete with ominous black pupil; the idea is that the hawks will see them as even more powerful predators and give them a wide berth.

If you have the space, you could also construct a feeding 'pergola' for smaller birds. This is simply a four-sided structure made from wooden trellis, with a piece of trellis nailed over it to make a 'roof'. The holes in the trellis are large enough for any of the smaller species to get through, but the structure works as an effective baffle for the hawk, who depends on an uninterrupted swoop to catch its prey. The structure is also light enough to be portable so you can move it, along with the feeders, to different spots around your garden.

A It may be a shock to see a garden bird caught and eaten before your eyes, but sparrowhawks need to feed just as blue tits do (and you probably don't have the same reaction when you see a blue tit chow down on a spider). Remember this sort of thing happens all the time, it is just that on this occasion you were there to witness it.

HAWKS IN THE CITY

Sparrowhawks (*Accipiter nisus*) and the larger and rarer peregrine (*Falco peregrinus*) have gradually moved into towns and suburban areas over the last two decades. With an abundance of potential nesting sites and plenty of food, both species have thrived in their urban surroundings. Of the two, the sparrowhawk is spotted much more frequently in gardens, while the powerful peregrine is a valued 'spot' for birdwatchers as it has acclimatized itself to living in the heart of the city, preying on urban pigeons and sometimes even swooping from the beams of construction cranes to catch them on the wing.

Peregrin falcon,
Falco peregrinus

I love badgers, but they're digging up the lawn; can I stop them?

YOU LIVE IN THE COUNTRY and overnight your lawn has been scored with large muddy trenches; badgers have been digging around for some of their favourite foods: worms, chafer grubs and other larvae. You like badgers, but you're keen on your lawn, too. Is there any benign way to stop them?

Some gardeners decide to prioritize badgers over their lawn, others go all out to exclude them with electric fences (one of the few commercial solutions that is a proven deterrent). Badgers (*Meles meles*) are some of the largest wild animals who will visit your garden. They're charming and interesting to watch, and they're also relatively easy to observe fairly close up. But they're also tenacious and very strong, with paws like heavily clawed shovels. Their interest is in the foods just underneath the surface: worms, leatherjackets (crane fly larvae) and chafer grubs. In dry weather, the damage they do to irrigated lawns tends to be worse than that done to dry ones; in the latter, the earthworms are closer to the surface and the watered ground is less difficult to dig than

When badgers treat your lawn as a buffet, the result can look as though someone's taken a mini-digger to it. To stop them, it's best to look at multiple strategies. Try removing the primary attraction, blocking off access and offering a feeding station with an even better menu.

hard-baked soil, so a watered lawn is offering the badgers an easier meal. They sometimes visit vegetable gardens and allotments for root crops, and they also enjoy fruits. They also eat other small mammals if they have the opportunity, including voles and hedgehogs.

◀ Badgers are determined and not easily deflected from their object – and if that's digging worms out of your lawn, you may need to try a number of different strategies to stop them.

GOING DOWN THE GARDEN TO EAT WORMS

Badgers love worms, particularly the common earthworm (*Lumbricus terrestris*); they can get through an estimated 200 per night. Short grass makes a happy hunting ground as, on a damp evening, earthworms come up to the surface in huge numbers. The heavy tread of an approaching badger may prompt a rapid retreat, but badgers push their snouts close to the soil's surface and literally suck the worm out. This leaves a characteristic pattern of round 'snuffle' holes for the gardener to discover the following day.

Try chicken wire

If they're concentrating on a specific area, you can peg chicken wire over the favoured digging patch. Use deep wire hoops to fasten down the edges so that they can't easily be pulled up. The wire won't hurt the badgers, but they don't like the feeling of it under their feet, and they can't get a purchase on areas of grass through the small holes.

Create a feeding station

If there's an alternative spot in your garden where you could feed the badgers, you can offer some delicacies that don't need to be dug for. Although some wildlife organizations don't recommend feeding badgers, you could take the view that your garden is inadvertently feeding them anyway so at least you can feed them in a way that suits you. You can buy specialist wildlife food or dried mealworms for badgers, but you don't really need to: they're keen on a wide variety of raw foods, including carrots, apples and unsalted raw peanuts. Don't offer 'human' foods or regular pet food. If you start feeding them your garden will become even more attractive – but a nightly smorgasbord may allay their interest in your lawn. A couple of handfuls of food nightly is plenty, and if it's in smallish pieces and scattered around, it will give you the best opportunity to watch as the badgers snuffle around collecting it.

Get rid of the food source

If one of the main attractions of the lawn are leatherjackets or chafer grubs, a partial solution may be to apply specific nematodes that will get rid of them. These are usually watered on to the lawn in spring, as the soil is warming up. If there aren't any grubs to be had, then the badgers won't dig for them – but bear in mind that experts estimate that earthworms make up somewhere between 50 and 80 per cent of the badger's diet, so even if you get rid of the grubs, they may dig anyway.

There's a wasp's nest in the garden; do I need to act?

YOU'VE NOTICED WASPS coming and going in and out of a large clump of ivy halfway up a tree. It seems pretty certain that they've built a nest there. Should you worry, or can it safely be left alone?

Like those of bumblebees, wasp colonies don't live very long: all the inhabitants with the exception of the young queens will die with the arrival of the first frost in autumn. And while in late summer the inhabitants may cause a nuisance when they buzz around in search of sugar, it's a small price to pay for having a whole nest of top-grade predators in the garden.

How the nest is made

With the coming of autumn and the death of the nest's inhabitants, it may be possible to climb up and retrieve the nest intact, and an undamaged wasp's nest is a really exceptional piece of construction.

When a queen wakes from hibernation in spring, she chooses a site and starts the build on her own, taking mouthfuls of wood – in gardens, fences and sheds are favourite sources – which she chews and mixes with her own saliva to make a paperlike paste (should you ever come across a building wasp, the chewing is surprisingly audible). She uses this to construct a central column, to support the nest, and anoints it with a chemical

A wasp's nest in the garden shouldn't be an automatic cause for alarm unless it's hidden somewhere where you may accidentally disturb it (wasps sometimes build their nests in holes in the ground). Once you're aware of a nest's location, if it's high up and won't inconvenience your own day-to-day activities, leave it in peace for its comparatively brief lifetime.

Common wasp queen (*Vespula vulgaris*) making a solo start on her nest. After she has made a few cells from chewed wood pulp, she will lay her first eggs, which will hatch into future worker wasps.

she secretes herself to repel ants (which sometimes predate wasps' nests). Then she starts to build cells around this centre. She continues to work on her own, constructing cells, then laying eggs in them, feeding the larvae which emerge and waiting until they grow and change into adult workers who can take over construction duties. Once she has created a sufficient workforce, she'll dedicate her time to laying eggs, while the workers continue to build cells, add layers to the nest construction,

and collect prey to feed the larvae. The colony grows quickly, housing as many as 10,000 wasps by mid-summer. By the beginning of August, unfertilized eggs will start to produce male wasps who will fly off to fertilize queens from other nests. Fertilized eggs, fed on a generous diet, will begin to hatch into the wasps which will become next year's queens. And all this takes place in a papery globe full of elegant hexagonal cells, about the size of a football.

ABOUT SWARMS

Common wasps will emerge in large numbers if the nest is under threat, but this is not a swarm. A harmed wasp, or one which has actually stung, will release a pheromone that warns the rest of the colony, a good reason why you should never swat a wasp: its co-workers are likely to emerge en masse to defend their territory.

A honeybee swarm happens for a completely different reason. When a honeybee hive grows past a certain size, the pheromones released by the queen, which 'rules' the hive, are no longer strong enough to reach all of the hugely increased population. Those bees to whom the signals don't reach respond to their

absence by creating a new queen, and this is the prompt for the old queen to depart the hive and look for new quarters, along with those bees who can fly. The bees who leave feed first, so they are full of honey and are looking for a home: well-fed and focused, they are unlikely to sting. If the queen needs to rest on the way, the other bees will cluster around her, and this creates the solid mass of bees that we call a swarm.

What should you do if you see a honeybee swarm? Don't approach it; instead, find the number of the nearest beekeeping association, who will send a beekeeper out to collect it and usher it into a vacant hive.

How can I help the underbug?

WHEN IT COMES TO WILDLIFE it's inevitable that the larger and more obviously eye-catching species tend to get the lion's share of attention. But it's the small ones that make up the largest number of garden residents. Given the alarming global fall in invertebrate numbers, how can you do your best for them in your own garden?

AEvery time you set up a little bit of different habitat in your garden, you're offering some space to a larger range of species than you may be aware of. And if you look beyond the few favoured groups such as bees and butterflies, you may discover some new favourites of your own to champion.

Just three per cent of species on the planet are vertebrates (creatures that have a backbone); plants and fungi account for another 17 per cent. And the remaining 80 per cent? They're the invertebrates (creatures lacking a backbone), without which the larger animal species would not exist and our living planet would be much less diverse. Learning a bit more about species you didn't know much about will increase your interest: invertebrate

lives are full of engaging details. Who wouldn't find the rather unloved earwig more interesting when you learn that she is a conscientious mother who spends hours cleaning her eggs, for example? Or be intrigued to be told that each egg laid by a female lacewing sways on its own threadlike stalk, like a minute toadstool?

The order of things

We tend to use the word 'bug' casually to indicate small invertebrates that we're not already familiar with. Technically we shouldn't: true bugs are an order, 'Hemiptera', which includes insects with piercing mouthparts, used to suck sap or the bodily fluids of other insects. Other orders include the true-flies (Diptera), Neuroptera, to which lacewings belong, bees (Hymenoptera), butterflies and moths (Lepidoptera), spiders (Araneae) and beetles (Coleoptera). But the term 'bug' has stuck – 'bug hotel', 'bug hunt' and so on – which is fine so long as we remember just how diverse these insects and other creatures really are.

The best way you can help the 'underbugs' is to acknowledge that

HARVESTMEN

Harvestmen might be considered classic cases of the underbug: they're eight-legged spider-like creatures (of the Opiliones order, which belong to the same group as arachnids) and which – along with craneflies and some species of long-legged spiders – you may know colloquially as daddy longlegs. The common harvestman (*Phalangium opilio*) is often spotted in the garden, hanging out wherever there's leaf litter, clumps of grass or foliage to offer some cover. Its small body (which doesn't have the visible division between thorax and abdomen that spiders do) seems to be slung under the joints of its immensely long legs – and it's the legs that make harvestmen particularly interesting. The second pair back from the head act as antennae and are acutely sensitive; you'll often see them waved in the air so that their owner can collect scent or sense movement around it. Despite their harmless appearance, harvestmen can chase down small prey, using hooks on their front legs to catch and hold it. If, on the other hand, a predator catches a harvestman by one of its long legs, the leg can be shed, but continues to twitch for a few seconds, possibly as a distraction device, to give its original owner the chance to get away.

every species has its place in the huge web of mutually dependent animals in the garden and to accept that with very few exceptions, they're not 'good' or 'bad' but are instead helping to keep the balance in a very complicated environment.

Look in different places

Make a field guide and a magnifying glass part of your ordinary gardening kit, alongside your trowel and secateurs, so that you can look at mini-beasts as you find them.
And make a point of looking in any corners that don't normally get much attention: your woodpile may shelter some interesting beetles as well as the familiar woodlice; a heap of pots left upside down is probably housing plenty of different spiders. In spring, turn over leaves and look for tiny mites and egg clutches. Some will be the size of pinheads, but a glass and a guide will help you to identify them. Get to know some of the less photogenic invertebrates and you'll find that they have their own appeal.

Q Is it okay to get rid of an ants' nest?

ANTS ARE ALWAYS PRESENT in the garden; if you look at any patch of ground for just a few moments, the common black ant (*Lasius niger*) will often be the first insect you see, bustling about on its invisible business. But if you find an ant's nest in your grass, at the edge of a border, or even in a plant pot, should you try to get rid of it?

Ants usually occupy a fairly neutral space in the gardener's consciousness: they tend to be neither loved, like bumblebees, nor much disliked, like aphids. Although there are actually over 60 different ant species found in the UK and nearly 200 in Europe, many are specialists that are only found in small areas of habitat. The common black ant remains the one that's seen around the garden most often.

Close encounters

You'll usually find the ants' nest by accident: at its worst the damage they do is limited to keeping water away from plant roots with their excavations; the latter, if they're taking place under a lawn, will also make the surface rather bumpy and uncomfortable to sit on. If the nest is in a plant pot and you're repotting, then you'll already have – unwittingly – forced them to move out. Shake as much of the soil, the ants and their eggs onto the ground and repot the plant with fresh soil; after a few minutes' confusion, you'll see the ants gathering up their eggs and scattering and, provided that you've shaken out the queen of the colony as well as the workers, they might regroup and find somewhere else to start. If you really want to shift a nest that's in the ground, buy a pack of the pathogenic nematodes that are available commercially and water the solution on. This doesn't kill the ants, but it will encourage them to

▼ The lumps and craters caused by the complex tunnels of an ants' nest can be annoying if you are lawn-proud – but they are generally best left alone.

move elsewhere. Don't follow the often-recommended advice to pour boiling water into an ants' nest – it's unnecessary cruel, and even if you aren't keen on them, remember that they are a popular food source higher up the web. If you find piles of excavated soil on the lawn where ants have been excavating, too, brush them across the grass before mowing. This is only a temporary solution, but it helps to avoid muddy patches afterwards.

Ants and aphids

Some gardeners object to ants on the grounds that they 'farm' aphids. In reality, the aphids were there anyway. The ants are enjoying the sweet liquid that they excrete and can sometimes

A Unless a nest is particularly unfortunately situated, it's generally best to leave it alone. If it's causing a real problem, you can encourage the ants to move elsewhere by watering the nest regularly.

be seen stroking the aphids to encourage them to produce more. It's true that they do sometimes act aggressively towards the aphids' enemies, such as ladybirds and ladybird and lacewing larvae, but unless your aphids are enjoying a population explosion (see pp82), the balance in the garden may take care of itself.

DO ANTS TASTE BAD?

There's an unusual behaviour that's been observed in a variety of garden birds, including sparrows, starlings and robins, called 'anting'. The bird takes an ant in its beak and rubs it all over the feathers of its wings and tail. Some scientists believed that the birds were using the formic acid contained in the ants as a natural treatment against parasites. One study of American blue jays (*Cyanocitta cristata*) published in 2008 concluded that the primary

reason for anting is that it makes the ant more palatable to eat. Some species of ants contain quite high levels of formic acid as a protection – they spray it when threatened – and this makes them more disagreeable to eat. But if the bird grabs the ant and forcibly rubs it, the ant discharges its supply of formic acid and then... bon appétit. Other alternative theories for anting are still being offered, though, so the discussion seems set to continue.

Apart from food, what other help does wildlife need in winter?

YOU'VE READ UP ON the best foods to offer wild birds in winter, your bee hotel is well established – and seems to have attracted some residents – and you've already moved a cluster of ladybirds to overwinter in the cool of the garage. Is there anything else you should be doing to help the wildlife in your garden?

Supply water

Birds bathe even more often in winter than summer to keep their plumage in top condition, so water is used for washing as well as drinking. In a large garden, leave two or three shallow basins of water in different spots. Refresh them daily so they are ice-free and don't spread disease. Use water from the water butt if you have one, the tap if you don't.

Don't cut back

Keep the secateurs indoors until later winter – thick, heavy growths of climbers such as ivy or evergreen clematis offer shelter (and in the case of ivy, food, too) in cold weather.

In flower beds, leave the dried stems of larger plants such as cardoons or fennel alone; they can supply shelter for overwintering insects (queen wasps often hibernate in them), and the plants can be tidied in spring. Cut stems can also be left in bundles in sheltered spots.

Leave the compost undisturbed

Although you're sometimes told to turn your compost heap 'with care' in winter, it's better if you can avoid turning it at all. Turning it carefully, while it may not harm any species such as slow worms,

Ivy,
Hedera helix

Make sure there's a supply of clean water, which is just as important as food, refrain from cutting back the borders, leave the compost heap unturned till spring and give existing leaf or wood piles a wide berth. Generally, deep winter isn't the best time of year to tidy.

frogs or hedgehogs that are hibernating in its depths, will still disturb them. Leave it alone until spring, when any residents will have woken up and departed – and which is also the best season to use the compost to mulch your borders.

Prepare for early nesters

Clear out and clean any nesting boxes in late autumn. Some birds start checking in to spring sites surprisingly early, particularly those that tend to produce multiple broods, such as blue tits, which may be hunting as early as January.

Think long-term

Winter is the best time for tree planting or hedge laying, and trees and hedges represent excellent future investments for wildlife. If you're thinking about adding either to your garden, this is the season to act.

BURNING ISSUE

Late autumn or the beginning of winter was usually the time of year you would collect all the unwanted wood and fallen leaves in the garden and have a bonfire. As environmental awareness has increased, the bonfire as a simple garden pleasure has become less popular: burning causes air pollution, and if left stacked for any time, the habitat a bonfire offers to wildlife may mean that it is sent up in smoke when the fire is lit. If the material you're planning to burn is healthy, you're missing an opportunity to repurpose it for wildlife, too: bundles of twigs or branches can be stacked as a mini woodpile; leaves can be piled together, offering cover for all kinds of species immediately and ultimately rotting down to make leaf mould, invaluable as mulch. What if you were planning to burn diseased plant material? Plants that suffer from various kinds of fungal, bacterial or viral diseases shouldn't be recycled, and a domestic compost heap probably won't get hot enough to kill off some of them on infected material. You can deliver waste to a local green composting centre; bury it (if you have the space and are up for the amount of digging involved) or, as a final option, burn it, provided you either have a garden incinerator or a large enough site to do it safely. If you do end up deciding on a bonfire, assemble the material immediately beforehand, and choose a still day so that wind doesn't blow the smoke around and annoy neighbours.

What natural food can I offer winter birds and wildlife?

WINTER CAN MEAN SLIM PICKINGS for all the wildlife in your garden. You may already have a feeding station for the birds, but can the plants you choose increase the supply of natural food available for them over the colder months?

Some plants offer an excellent autumn and winter payoff for wildlife with their seeds, fruit and berries. Choose carefully and leave any cutting back of seedheads until spring. If you have an oak or a beech in the garden, acorns and beechnuts are an added bonus for many species.

Plants to choose

Teasel and sunflower seedheads are famously popular with goldfinches and sparrows, but other plants to consider for their seeds as well as their flowers include knapweeds, lemon balm and lavender. Many ornamental grasses are also very generous with their seed production. Add in hips and berries from roses, ivy or holly and your garden can offer a lot of winter food. Don't forget to put out water, too.

MAINTAINING A LARDER

A number of garden bird species are provident enough to hide away stores of food for winter. Jays top the list, with an insatiable appetite for acorns: a single bird may hide up to 5,000 acorns a year, burying them or secreting them in trees. They carry them back to their home territories, which may be several kilometres from the parent oaks – so if you find oak seedlings when there are no oaks anywhere near, a jay may have left part of its cache behind. Nuthatches (*Sitta europaea*) are also hoarders: they collect and hide nuts from garden feed stations, eating more when they are being observed and hiding stores when they don't think they're being watched. Birds also steal caches of food: great tits are notorious for observing food being hidden and then swooping in on it when the original 'owner' flies off.

How can I keep squirrels from emptying my bird feeders?

I WANT TO FEED THE BIRDS, but I've got some outstandingly agile and determined grey squirrels regularly visiting my garden. Is there any way I can see them off, or at least ensure that they don't get more than their fair share?

There are two options, one perhaps more fun than the other. You can buy some very effective squirrel-proof feeders. Or you can force your squirrels to work for their nuts by setting up an obstacle course which it will take their utmost agility to overcome.

TRY AN OBSTACLE COURSE

While you may not ultimately defeat a determined squirrel, this route makes for good entertainment: ignore the various common-sense commercial solutions and use your own imagination to set up a series of homemade obstacles, and see how the squirrel gets on! There are plenty of YouTube videos you can use for inspiration if your imagination runs low. Loose rings and tubes placed along the unstable washing line from which the feeders are hung make good starter obstacles.

Proof against squirrels

An old word-of-mouth remedy suggests mixing chilli powder with bird food: birds aren't affected by chilli but squirrels, like most mammals, are. This doesn't seem the kindest route, however, and there are a number of commercial feeding options advertised as 'squirrel proof'. Weight-sensitive hanging feeders which close when something over a certain heft lands on them seem to work well against squirrels, although if you also want to discourage pigeons and magpies their lighter weight may not be sufficient for the feeder to shut up shop. Wire cage feeders with a mesh fine enough to exclude squirrels can be used on the ground – although there's anecdotal evidence that if you also have visiting badgers a cage may not be the best choice, because the badgers will dig the ground around it to raw earth.

Will weeding between paving slabs harm wildlife?

WHEN YOU HAVE A PATIO or yard laid with paving slabs, bricks or even crazy paving, it may not immediately look like a very promising habitat for wildlife. Does anyone live in the gaps and, if so, will weeding between the stones disrupt them?

Even if you prefer to weed, the channels between paving can become nesting sites to some species, such as solitary mining bees, which like a little bare soil to set up their nests. If you want some plants you can wait for some to arrive on their own. Unless you want a lot of dandelions, though, you may want to make your own selection.

What kind of paving?

In a new place where you're laying paving yourself, you can leave small spaces between the pavers deliberately: even a 1–2cm (1in) gap will work well as a growing area for a whole host of pollinator-friendly plants. Crazy paving lends itself particularly well to this – you can leave small holes between pieces to make additional growing spaces.

If you've inherited a paved space and the stones or slabs are mortared in, check the condition of the mortar: over time, it usually cracks and degrades, and it may be easier to ease chunks of it out than start again.

Once a paved space is planted up, pull out or use a weeding knife to limit plant spread or take out any weeds you don't want.

Signs of life below ground

If the paving is laid directly on soil, or on a bed of sand over soil, some species will create burrows in the soil with entrances in the gaps between the stones. If you spot tiny heaps of soil near or alongside the channels, it's a sign that someone such as the early mining bee (*Andrena haemorrhoa*) has been digging. You may also sometimes see a leaf pulled halfway down into the ground – the sign of an anecic earthworm collecting its next meal.

Stones laid edge-to-edge or mortared together aren't very hospitable (although plants will still 'take' in surprisingly tiny gaps), but slightly wider spaces left between slabs, with soil or sand rather than mortar between them, are both plant and wildlife friendly.

FIVE WILDLIFE-FRIENDLY PLANTS
TO GROW BETWEEN PAVING

Many herbs that pollinators like will 'take' when planted between slabs or brick pavers, but there are plenty of other options, too.

Welsh poppy (*Papaver cambricum*) This four-petalled yellow poppy on thin, wiry stems is happy in shade and will self-seed between bricks or paving slabs or in cracks in walls. Flowering between June and August, it's popular with pollinators. Flowers can grow as tall as 50cm (20in).

Origanum vulgare **'Compactum'** This compact marjoram, which grows in a small clump or mound, is ideal for filling in a small gap where a paving corner is cracked or missing. Strongly fragrant with small sprays of pale pink flowers over a long season, lasting well into autumn. Up to 15cm (6in) height.

Thymus serpyllum **'Pink Chintz'** A creeping thyme with heads of pinkish-mauve flowers which will quickly colonize the cracks in paving, is tough enough to stand a certain amount of footfall (and will smell delicious when trodden on) and which has a strong appeal for bees. Can grow to 10cm (4in) in height but can be cut back hard as necessary.

Erigeron karvinskianus Another plant which bees like, the Mexican fleabane has a long flowering season and will form pretty sprawling mats across paved areas. Its daisy-like flowers open white but gradually turn pink. Up to 15cm (6in) height.

Lobularia maritima **'Rosie O'Day'** A highly scented sweet alyssum with flowers that open white but gradually turn rose-pink in colour with a yellow eye. Popular with hoverflies and a number of smaller insects. With regular deadheading it will flower indefatigably in summer. Up to 10cm (4in) height.

Creeping thyme,
Thymus serpyllum

I cut back a bush full of caterpillars – can they be saved?

YOU WERE CUTTING BACK a patch of nettles that was spreading from its usual spot behind your compost heap, and you belatedly noticed that a couple of the plants were heaving with furry black caterpillars. What are they, and now you've cut their host plant down, is it possible to move them?

From one nettle to another

Peacock caterpillars are relatively easy to move, as stinging nettles are so very common. Gently roll the caterpillars off the cut plant and encourage them onto the leaves of one that's still standing. Alternatively, take the cut nettles and lay them directly alongside the growing ones: caterpillars aren't as helpless as they look, and will readily climb up a new stem provided that it's nearby.

If there aren't any standing nettles, it's probably best to leave the cut plants lying, complete with caterpillars. There's a chance that they might be very near their pupating stage, in which case they may survive. Don't go hunting for an alternative

They sound like the caterpillars of the peacock butterfly (*Aglais io*). As adults, they'll have the familiar vivid wings with big violet-and-black eyespots in each corner. The caterpillars are also handsome, gleaming black all over, with black spikes and a scattering of white spots. If you can find some nettles still standing, you should be able to gently transfer them.

nettle patch outside your garden: as a general policy, it's always best to avoid moving species outside your boundary. This may sound unnecessarily strict, but if you stick to it, there's never any chance that you will accidentally spread disease or unwelcome species into the outside world.

◀ The black spines of the peacock caterpillar help to protect it from many predators, although it is a common prey of various species of parasitic wasp.

CAN A MOTH REMEMBER BEING A CATERPILLAR?

It may seem that caterpillars don't share anything at all with their adult form: the sombre caterpillar of a painted lady, for example, gives no hint of its colourful adulthood, nor does the chunky little all-green larva of the common blue offer any clues as to the pure-blue beauty that will eventually emerge from the pupal case. The pupal stage, the in-between one, sees the most complete transformation imaginable. In order to achieve it, the caterpillar shrinks and sheds its skin, and its organs liquefy; the 'imaginal' or adult cells that exist somewhere inside this mix then rework the caterpillar soup into the form of a butterfly or moth. A study published in 2008 established – almost unbelievably – that some sensations experienced by caterpillars seemed to carry on in the memories of the transformed adult. In an experiment at Georgetown University in the US, scientists gave mildly aversive shocks to caterpillars of the tobacco hornworm moth while exposing them to a specific odour. As adults, they found that moths still avoided the smell which, when they were larvae, they had associated with the shocks. At some level, they seemed to be remembering their lives as caterpillars.

Tobacco hornworm,
Manduca sexta

Adult moth

Larva

Fussy eaters

While a number of species of butterfly also favour nettles at their caterpillar stage, others may be less easily satisfied. Nettles are very common (and, perhaps not coincidentally, peacock butterflies are also quite common over most of Europe and the UK), but some species at their caterpillar stage have very specific food tastes and simply shifting them to the leaves of a nearby but unrelated plant won't work. You're unlikely to accidentally cut down an alder buckthorn tree, the leaves of which are the sole food eaten by the caterpillar of the brimstone butterfly (*Gonepteryx rhamni*), but then you aren't likely to have the tree in your garden at all, so your garden won't attract brimstones to lay eggs. For some favoured caterpillar food plants, see pp47.

Chapter 5

The Bigger Picture

How can my small garden be a wildlife haven?

THERE'S A LOT OF GLOOM IN THE NEWS about wildlife, to the point where you may begin to feel that any personal, individual efforts aren't really worth making. Can your small garden make a difference to the overall wildlife picture?

Anywhere that people garden is a potential space that nature can use: put plants into the ground, or even into containers, and you've formed a habitat. And if you aim to garden in a wildlife-friendly way it maximizes the potential your space has for nature. Unlike farmland, the garden doesn't have to do another job, but it can be dedicated to wildlife interests. Nor do you need much space, especially since one of the biggest concerns to ecologists is the steep decline in the number of insects, many of which don't need a lot of room to shelter, feed or breed. And when it comes to larger species, one study established that the density of the bird population in urban Sheffield was six times that of the average bird population in the UK. Thousands of gardens add up to something quite significant: in 2006, it was estimated that if you added up the total area of all gardens in the UK, you would arrive at close to 100,000 acres (433,000 ha) – that's an area one fifth the size of Wales.

◁ If the ground space in your garden is limited, think vertical. Climbers are often a good option, or you can think creatively: this wall-mounted pallet has been used to house clustered containers.

Additions for wildlife

So gardens matter, however small. If you're reassured by this but still feel that you're not doing enough, consider whether you're able to extend your own garden's wildlife value further by adding a pond or some other water feature; planting a tree, even a small one; swapping a fence for a hedge; or simply ensuring that every plant you grow has a wildlife value for something out there. Bear in mind, when you're thinking about the latter, that it doesn't necessarily mean that you have to be a purist about growing 'native' plants – some 'alien' plants may offer unexpected benefits to local wildlife,

Yes! Your garden is important, as are all the other gardens nearby. Wildlife doesn't recognize the boundaries that people do – think of the landscape that you would see from above and imagine all those dozens of gardens, each a single piece of a bigger mosaic and each playing its own part in sustaining diverse species.

such as helping to extend the flowering season or by providing valuable evergreen cover in winter.

ONE 'ORDINARY' GARDEN

Don't underestimate the riches that can be found in an ordinary garden. In the UK, Jennifer Owen, a naturalist and university lecturer, made a long-term study of her suburban garden in Leicestershire. She had previously lived in Uganda and Sierra Leone and after more than a decade away she was keen to look at the diversity a less exotic garden might offer. She published the results after she had been studying her garden for 15 years, and again after 30 years. Across that time, she identified 2,673 different species, breaking the total down as 474 plants, 1,997 insects, over 138 invertebrates (such as spiders and woodlice), 7 mammals and 54 birds – a triumph of small-scale wildlife gardening. Over the decades she noted a general decline in diversity, attributing it to an increasing shortage of neighbouring habitats (underlining how important it is that every scrap of land possible should be enlisted to support wildlife). These totals aren't particularly high: in global terms, the UK has an impoverished flora and fauna; similar like-for-like studies made in parts of Europe reached substantially higher numbers.

Q If you cut down a tree, should you put a new one in its place?

EVEN SMALL TREES IN A GARDEN offer high value when it comes to food and shelter for wildlife. But sometimes losing a tree can't be avoided: it may be unsafe or diseased, it may have been planted in the wrong place or outgrown its space, or it may have to be sacrificed to give other trees around it enough room. If you need to take a tree out of your garden, is it best to replace it?

A If you have a tree that needs to be felled, assess the space and the reason it had to go before deciding what should replace it. Ideally, a tree should be replaced with a tree, although if the reason the first was cut down was honey fungus or another disease, you may not be able to put a new one on the same site.

Why was it felled?

If your tree was sited too near a building or outgrew the space available for it, think carefully before you replace it. Something smaller may grow happily in the same space, or it may be more sensible to site a replacement – large or small – in a more open site. If the felled tree died as a result of honey fungus, a new one should be sited well away from where

HOW WILL IT LOOK?

One common reason for felling a tree is that it grew larger than expected. Most people look up height and spread before planting a tree; what they don't realize is what that height and spread will look like, even if there is technically room for it. Photograph the potential site and superimpose a scale cutout of the adult tree you're considering over it. This will give you a more realistic idea of how it will look.

the old one was removed, and you should choose a species which has a lesser susceptibility to the disease You can find full lists of these online, but try something like the black walnut (*Juglans nigra*), pictured.

Why is peat prohibited?

IF YOU WERE TO GO BACK to the gardens of the 1960s and 1970s, you'd find the majority of gardeners using a lot of peat in their potting compost mixes and as a soil improver: it was valued because of its ability to hold water, as well as its sterility. Why is its use frowned on now, and what should you use instead?

Peat bogs replace themselves very slowly, at the rate of a single millimetre of depth per year, which is a powerful argument for leaving peat in the ground. For the gardener, the job previously done by peat can largely be filled by peat-free potting composts and well-rotted compost (and sometimes leaf mould, too). Even specialist plants that would naturally grow in peat bogs, such as carnivorous plants, can be grown in peat-free mixes using a combination of sphagnum moss, lime-free grit or sand, perlite and fine bark.

Peat comes from peat bogs – very specific habitats which are both wet and very low in oxygen. They are valuable absorbers of carbon, which stays in the bog rather than being released into the atmosphere as carbon dioxide. Apart from their value as carbon sponges, bogs are also home to large numbers of habitat-specific species, from gnats to butterflies.

CAN I USE COIR INSTEAD?

Coir is sometimes proposed as an alternative to peat. It's made from the compressed fibres of coconut husks, and it's a natural waste product from coconut farming. It retains water well and can be a good addition to heavier clay soils, breaking them up and helping to aerate plant roots. Because it's a waste product it's often assumed that coir is environmentally friendly, but this leaves out the fact that it is largely produced in Asia, so has to be shipped a very long way to reach gardens in Europe. Also its production uses a great deal of water, so the choice between peat and coir suddenly seems much less obvious. For the domestic gardener, home-made compost is a much better answer.

Can I have a cat and a bird table?

YOU LOVE YOUR CAT and you also enjoy the presence of birds in your garden, so you're in a difficult position: there's no denying that pet cats kill a lot of garden birds (a study by the Mammal Society estimated 55 million per year in the UK alone), as well as high numbers of small rodents, frogs, bats and other animals. Do cats have an impact on bird populations overall, and is there anything you can do to stop your cat's predatory habits in the garden?

A few cats aren't interested in hunting – if yours is one of them, count yourself lucky, but work on the assumption that other cats may visit your garden. Site your bird table away from any spots a cat could use for concealment. You can buy a baffle to use under the table or improvise one: an upturned cone or biscuit tin pierced with a central hole and placed around the support pole should work, as will grease smeared onto the pole to discourage climbing.

Belling the cat

If your cat catches birds, you can help prevent this by fitting it with a quick-release collar with two bells. This is safe for the cat – if it catches on anything the collar will unfasten – and it will limit the cat's ability to stalk birds without being noticed (skilled hunters can sometimes learn to move in a way that stops a single bell ringing, but this is harder to do with two). A cat bib, which is a piece of fabric fastened around the neck –

It's a vexed subject and non-cat lovers are usually quick to point the finger when it comes to news about the falling populations of wild birds. If you want a bird table, be responsible: there are steps you can take to limit the opportunity your cat has to take garden birds, so make sure that you've covered the basics.

DO WE UNDERSTAND THE EFFECT CATS HAVE ON BIRDS?

We know that cats catch birds, and that young birds, with less mobility, stand a higher chance of being caught than others. Some studies have argued that cats tend to predate sick or weak birds and thus, despite the high quantity of birds taken, don't actually make much impact on wild bird populations. Others have come to the opposite conclusion. But a study made by the University of Sheffield in 2013 seemed to argue that the cat vs. bird situation was more complicated than previously thought. A stuffed cat was placed near a blackbird's nest for 15 minutes; the effect on the parent birds was to send them into a frenzy of alarm calls and protective displays. This in turn disrupted their work of collecting and ferrying food to their young in the nest and continued to upset them for an hour and a half after the 'cat' had been removed.

(Control studies used a stuffed squirrel – also a possible predator for nesting blackbirds – and a stuffed rabbit, a species that wouldn't pose a threat.) Studies of the nesting sites over the following couple of days showed that a quarter of them had had visits from magpies or crows; a result which may have meant that the parent birds' frantic efforts to drive the stuffed cat away drew the attention of other predators to a nest that up to that point had remained unnoticed. This idea was reinforced by the controls: the parent blackbirds had ignored the stuffed squirrel and rabbit, and their nests weren't predated. It was a limited study, but it suggests that the effects of cats on garden birds aren't confined to direct predation – they may also disrupt feeding of the young birds and, by their mere presence, encourage visits by other predators.

it looks very much how it sounds – seems to be an even more effective deterrent: it disrupts a cat's ability to pounce without limiting its other activities. During the nesting season and particularly when young birds are fledging, try to limit your cat's outdoor time. Keep it indoors overnight, from an hour before sunset (this will also protect bats emerging from their roosts), and as far as possible during the day except when you're outdoors yourself, especially if you know you have nests in the garden.

What's the best nature-friendly garden boundary?

PERHAPS YOUR GARDEN FENCE is coming to the end of its life and you'll need a new boundary for your garden, or maybe you've moved into a new space and need to create a garden 'divider' from scratch. Fence or hedge: what's the best choice and why?

In the countryside hedgerows have become increasingly rare, so the best thing to redress the balance is to grow one in your own garden. They offer food and shelter for all kinds of species, and can also offer a safe route for wildlife moving from one spot to another.

Hedging

Conifer hedges have limited appeal for wildlife, while other berried evergreens, such as yew, are popular with nesting birds, which also enjoy the berries. Deciduous, multi-species hedges are generally considered to have the most to offer. If there's an existing hedge but it's sparse or made up of a single species, consider introducing some other plants – ivy or old man's beard (*Clematis vitalba*), for example.

Hedge trimming should happen over winter, leaving plenty of buffer around the nesting season, which may start as early as February. Some hedge plants flower and produce berries on two-year wood, and these should be trimmed only every other year – this will ensure they have the chance to flower and produce berries better in their untrimmed year.

It depends on what kind of space you have and how much time you can invest. The benefits of a hedge vary according to which trees or shrubs it's composed of: some are better in wildlife terms than others. If you're limited to a fence or wall, it can be made more wildlife-friendly with climbers or wall-trained shrubs such as cotoneaster.

Fences with plants

If you can't have a hedge but do have either a fence or a wall, look at what you can grow up it to increase its wildlife potential. Ivy is always a good choice, although it will only bear berries once it reaches the top. Some *Clematis* varieties are worthwhile because they offer flowers at the end of winter, when they're particularly valued by insects such as queen bumblebees emerging from hibernation.

GROWING A NATIVE HEDGE

A hedge made up of mixed native plants certainly offers a lot for wildlife, but it is very fast-growing and vigorous, so only plant one if you have the space to let it fill out. Young plants or whips are available both from nurseries and by mail order, and are usually sold in quantities that allow between three and five plants per metre (1yd) or seven plants for a double row, which will give a dense hedge quicker.

The 'recipe' is usually three plants of the same species and one each of two different species to each metre (or yard) of ground. Usually around half the plants you receive will be a single species – most commonly hawthorn (*Crataegus monogyna*) – while the balance will be made up of a mix of other species. Mixed hedges potentially contain a whole range of plants including, but not limited to, blackthorn (*Prunus spinosa*), common beech (*Fagus sylvatica*), hornbeam (*Carpinus betulus*), hazel (*Corylus avellana*), common dogwood (*Cornus sanguinea*), field maple (*Acer campestre*) and dog rose (*Rosa canina*). A good variety ensures that the hedge will offer year-round cover as well as a range of fruits and nuts for food. The ground for a new hedge should be prepared carefully,

Common beech,
Fagus sylvatica

large stones removed and some compost or leaf mould dug in. Plant the whips in a single row, varying the species combinations along the hedge's length – this will avoid a uniform impression when it is fully grown. If planting a double row, stagger them. Use a line to check that you're planting straight and trim the whips back to 15–30cm (6–12in) once planted to encourage bushy growth. If you angle them slightly as you put them in, it will help ensure that your hedge isn't thin at the base. Trim regularly for the first year or two so that it remains compact and doesn't become straggly.

Blackthorn,
Prunus spinosa

Can off-street parking be wildlife friendly?

WHEN YOUR FRONT GARDEN has to accommodate a parked car, does it mean you have to give up on a wildlife-friendly approach, or can the same space double up as garden and car park?

What to park on

Cars don't need to be parked on solid areas of paving. For example, you can make a perfectly workable parking space with just two strips for a car's wheels to rest on, although obviously, the broader the strips, the easier it will be to park. Bricks, gravel or matrix pavers, which offer a solid structure but have hollows that can be filled with gravel or even soil, are all permeable and will allow rainwater to soak into the ground. Brick pavers will need a base of compacted aggregate to ensure they don't sink, but matrix pavers and gravel can be placed directly on firmed soil. There are also mesh and grid products available that will reinforce

There are plenty of creative ways to plant a space that also has to serve as off-street parking. It's not just the wildlife that will benefit from this pocket of green: you'll also be helping to mitigate against flash flooding and the 'heat island' effect, in which towns are warmer than the countryside around them as the result of concentrated human activities.

grass so that you can park on it without reducing it to an earthy mush. Once you've decided on the material, positioning and installation method of the 'tracks', you're free to design the rest of the space.

◀ A good example of an off-street parking scheme which offers plenty of space for a car and a generous amount of planting.

CONCRETE JUNGLE

What about a front 'garden' that's already been concreted over? If you aren't able to break up the concrete (if you're living in rented accommodation, say, and your landlord won't give permission), think about planting up containers instead. The more you have, the more rainwater they'll intercept to help slow storm water from reaching public drains, and you can choose a variety of plants that will give pollinators good reason to visit: from herbs and perennials that will cover a long flowering season to climbers that can scramble over a porch or fence and offer some potential cover and food for birds and insects.

What to plant

Look at the available area when the car is parked. Maybe you have enough space left over to create borders around the edges – if you're lucky, there may even be enough room to plant some shrubs as well as smaller plants. Wildlife-friendly stalwarts such as pyracantha, ivy and honeysuckle are all tough enough to cope without constant, dedicated care (front gardens don't tend to encourage the same relaxed, do-a-bit, rest-a-bit gardening sessions that back gardens – quieter and more secluded – do, so you may want to go for some easy-care options). Plant quite densely, going into the corners, to make the best use of all the available space. Perennial herbs, such as lavender, rosemary and fennel (the bronze variety, *Foeniculum vulgare* 'Purpureum', is especially striking) will all grow happily in poor soil and a sunny position, only needing an occasional trim to keep them in good condition, plus they're popular with insects, and smell great!

Under-car planting

Even the 'central reservation' between two parking strips can be planted up if the car isn't there constantly. You need low-growing, resilient plants for this space, such as creeping thymes *Thymus serpyllum* or the *Thymus* Coccineus Group (both have pink flowers and bees love them), bugle (*Ajuga reptans*) or creeping Jenny (*Lysimachia nummularia*).

Bugle,
Ajuga reptans

Can I garden without chemicals?

YOUR AIM IS TO GARDEN without using any harmful chemicals at all. But does chemical-free gardening mean that you'll have to sacrifice plant condition?

Dealing with pests

If you've decided to go chemical-free, there are a number of different ways to control the populations of invertebrates you don't want. Some, such as aphids, can be washed off plants with water, or squashed by hand. Slugs and snails can be collected from plants (night-time slug-catching expeditions with a torch are often exciting for children, enabling you to double up pest control with family time). If you're hard-hearted, you can leave your catch in a bucket of water, then tip the whole thing onto the compost heap. If you don't like the

idea, you can deposit slugs and snails on the compost heap and live in hope that they'll stay there – although if it's less than 20m (65ft) away from where they were originally picked up, they may find their way back.

Encourage predators

Give some natural predators encouragement to do their work with plenty of pollinating plants: wasps and lacewings are both keen predators. Lacewing and ladybird larvae, as well as ladybird adults, can, and do, eat huge quantities of aphids. You can also introduce pathogenic nematodes: the fix you can't see. Used carefully, they can be effective at keeping the populations of all kinds of pests, from slugs to vine weevils, down.

Dealing with weeds

The harder work for you may come with weed control. If you don't use herbicides, the only alternative is to deal with weeds manually, by pulling them out, hoeing or smothering them with thick layers, at least 10cm (4in), of mulch. In the latter case, take care not to pile mulch up too closely around the plant you're protecting, as it may cause the stem to rot. Manual weeding, with

▼ Birds eat plenty of grubs, caterpillars, slugs and snails. The more encouragement they're given to visit your garden, the more they'll help out.

a hoe or your hands, is either tedious or meditative depending on your mindset, but short and regular sessions will ensure that you stay on top of the more biddable weeds.

Weed barriers

The big guns of the weed world, such as horsetail or ground elder, may need more forceful treatment: their roots are very deep and far reaching, which means that, while you may dig them out as far as you can, you're unlikely to be able to eliminate them altogether. Purpose-made root barriers, made from a tough material that won't rot and often used to stop plants like bamboo from spreading out of control, can also be used if these weeds are causing a real problem in specific areas of your garden. The weeds will

A Gardeners tended their gardens for centuries without insecticides; doing without them shouldn't lead to too many compromises. You may have to be patient and learn to tolerate a few unwanted invertebrates while their natural predators come to full strength. If you've used herbicides in the past, the no-chemical route will mean that your relationship with weeds will get more physical, too.

need to be dug out as far as possible first: the barriers are then sunk vertically into the ground along the edges of areas you want to protect.

'NATURAL' DOESN'T NECESSARILY MEAN HARMLESS

You've probably seen the many recipes available for home-made 'all-natural' insecticides or herbicides that are made from a range of ingredients, from neem oil to infusions of tobacco. And if your idea of an insecticide is something that comes in a commercial spray with warnings on the label, 'natural' may sound reassuring. But the definition of an insecticide or a herbicide is something that kills an insect or a plant; it doesn't say anything about how it does it, and 'natural' remedies may have effects that aren't predictable in your garden. If you've decided against using chemicals, abandon the home lab, too, and look to the predators in your garden to deal with the insects you don't want and to your own physical activity to get rid of the plants that aren't welcome.

Are all trees equally good for wildlife?

TREES SUPPLY A HABITAT all of their own, so they are a good addition to any garden. And they can be suited to the space available; most gardens will have enough room for at least a single, small tree and maybe more. But how various are their wildlife benefits?

Every tree has something to offer wildlife. Oak and beech trees, for example, may support hundreds of species but are usually too large and too slow-growing to be practical choices for all but the biggest and longest-owned gardens. Plenty of smaller trees will grow quickly enough for you to plant and see the benefits in just a few years.

The bird cherry *Prunus padus* 'Colorata' has appealing pale pink flowers that stand out against its dark foliage.

People in modern society move more times in their lives than they did in the past, so when it comes to choosing a tree or trees you may need to look beyond your time in your garden and think in terms of the future as well as the present. Choose the largest tree that will fit in your space but pay attention to the mature height and spread to make sure it can stay where it's been planted. If you only have space for a smaller tree, remember that it has the advantage that it's easier to look closely and spot the bird and insect life going on in the bark and among the branches.

Plant for posterity

Of course if you have a big garden, you could always think in terms of going really large and planting for generations to come. The trees of the future had to start somewhere, and if you have the space to plant a tree, choose carefully, and watch it grow for as long as you're there. Oak trees can live for over 500 years, so seeing one through its first 10 to 20 years is a privilege, even though a young oak may not bring you the evident wildlife benefits of, say, a mature rowan.

FIVE GOOD WILDLIFE TREES FOR A SMALL GARDEN

A smaller garden may only have room for one tree, so make sure it's a good one. All of these are small to medium in size, are winners in terms of the quantity of wildlife, from insects to birds, that they attract, and look appealing, too. Incidentally, if you're choosing a berry-bearing tree for birds, they tend to favour orange or red berries over pink ones.

Sorbus aucuparia 'Fastigiata' Height 4–8m (13–26ft), spread 2.5–4m (8–13ft). A columnar-shaped rowan tree which will fit well into a narrow space. It has creamy-white scented flowers followed by generous clusters of bright red berries.

Crab apple (*Malus sylvestris*) Height 8–12m (26–40ft), spread 4–8m (13–26ft). Crab apples have a neat, rounded shape, with pinkish-white blossom in spring followed by small fruit, particularly favoured by blackbirds, thrushes and starlings.

Amelanchier laevis 'Snowflakes' Height 4–8m (13–26ft), spread 4–8m (13–26ft). Very pretty foliage, copper when it first emerges, turning first green through summer, then a red-streaked gold in autumn. Large scented flowers are followed in summer by sweet, blue-black berries.

▲ As well as residents, including starlings and blackbirds, winter visitors such as this waxwing (*Bombycilla garrulus*) also enjoy winter berries.

Prunus padus 'Colorata' Height 8–12m (26–40ft), spread 4–8m (13–26ft). A variety of bird cherry with reddish-purple leaves, pale pink flower clusters and small black fruits.

Elder (*Sambucus nigra*) Height 4–8m (13–26ft), spread 2.5–4m (8–13ft). A familiar sight from many wild hedgerows, elder trees are also excellent for attracting wildlife to the garden. Umbels of sweet-smelling creamy flowers act as insect magnets; they are followed by sprays of black berries.

Will my neighbour's gardening habits affect wildlife in my garden?

YOU'VE STUDIED THE BEST PLANTS and practice for wildlife gardening, you've dug a pond, and you're happy that you're on the right track to maximizing your garden's biodiversity. Your neighbours, though, tend to start pruning their climbers just as the nesting season is getting going and don't seem to share your favoured chemical-free approach. Will their gardening habits create a problem on your side of the fence?

Any gardening at all is good for wildlife – it supplies an environment which at least some species can call home – so the fact that your neighbours enjoy gardening is a plus, even if you don't share values. There's not much evidence that pesticide use in a neighbouring garden will have a direct and damaging effect on yours, either.

Gardening is a very inclusive passion and you're all gardeners, so it's better to concentrate on what you have in common than your differences. Make friends, discuss gardening and, eventually, you'll be able to share views on different gardening styles. Don't be patronizing or question how your neighbours go about maintaining their garden. You're more likely to convert them to your point of view through friendly overtures and informal chatting over coffee.

▼ Since wildlife doesn't observe human boundaries, what happens over the garden fence will have an effect on your garden – but any garden is intrinsically a plus for wildlife.

 Encourage fellow gardeners to enjoy some of the smaller visitors to the garden, such as hoverflies and bee flies, which often get less attention.

Softly, softly

Remember that their garden is their affair, however strongly you feel about it. You're free to talk about your own wildlife interests, explain that you don't use chemicals, offer a gift from your vegetable garden and listen to what they have to say.

If they have habits that really bother you, such as chemical spraying close to the boundary with your garden, when you've established good relations you'll be able to ask if they can maybe spray on still days only: you hate to think of the valuable hoverflies and bees that visit your own garden being harmed. Talk about the nesting habits of robins, and how great it is that it's finally been made illegal to disturb nesting birds. Bring out your knowledge of the minutiae of bee and hoverfly lives, explain that you counted 10 different kinds of bee in your garden last year, ask them if they'd like you to show them some of the most appealing features of your favourites. Wear them down with charm, and eventually you may be able to bring them around to your own way of thinking about wildlife-friendly gardening.

COMBINING FORCES

Maybe, instead of a neighbour whose gardening habits set your teeth on edge, you have one who thinks very much as you do. If you are both keen on wildlife and enthusiastic about maximizing the diversity in your gardens, looking at what each garden can offer and ensuring that they complement each other is a good strategy, especially if neither garden is large. You're unlikely to want to share everything, but if your neighbour's garden has a decent-sized woodpile, you might consider devoting the equivalent space in yours to a stone cairn, for example. And sharing can make for useful economies of space: having a joint leaf pile in one garden, say, can free up a corner in the other for some extra plants chosen specifically for pollinators. It's a communal way of thinking, but the bonus can be that the wildlife gets a double-sized plot with as many different features as can possibly be fitted in.

How can I be sure that the plants I buy are pesticide-free?

YOU HAVE A NO-CHEMICAL RULE in your garden. But it's been reported that plants available in nurseries are raised with pesticides and that traces may remain when you bring them home which, if true, is bad news for the bees and other insects that will visit them. How can you be certain that you're not accidentally bringing pesticides into your garden?

Questions raised over whether or not plants grown for and stocked by nurseries have been treated with pesticides were partly spurred by a study from the Universities of Sussex and Padua in 2017 which tested a number of nursery-purchased plants, many of which were sold as pollinator-friendly. The results were worrying and attracted a lot of publicity: a high proportion of the plants bought showed traces of a wide range of fungicides and

RAISE FROM SEED

Growing plants from seed can become addictive: it's cheap, which gives you lots of opportunity to experiment; it leaves you with a generous supply of plants, which, in turn, offers plenty of opportunity for you to swap seedlings and young plants with other gardeners; and it means you can be absolutely certain that the bee-friendly plants that you're raising are just that. You don't need a greenhouse or any special equipment, just a sunny windowsill, some seed compost and some trays or small pots.

Some species are easier – and speedier – to germinate than others, and a few need rather specific conditions. It's worth reading up on what you plan to grow before you plant to check, for example, whether the seedlings will be happy to be moved or should be planted where you want them to end up, or whether larger, harder seeds such as those of sweet peas need nicking with a knife (a practice called 'chipping'), to make it easier for them to germinate.

pesticides, neonicotinoids among them, in some cases in quite high quantities. Neonicotinoid pesticides have been proven to damage wild bee populations and are widely banned in Europe.

Where pesticide residues come from

The journey of a plant to the nursery where it is sold can be quite a long one – a lot of large nurseries and chains don't raise the plants themselves but buy them in, from a variety of sources, both national and international. Pesticide residues can linger in the compost plants are grown in and can be long-lasting in the plants themselves, and laws about pesticide use vary between countries. The huge market that supplies nurseries with ornamental plants means that the methods by which those plants have been grown are inherently hard to track. When a plant is labelled bee- or pollinator-friendly, it indicates that the species of plant is good for pollinators, but it doesn't tell you anything about the conditions in which that particular plant was raised.

Best sources

It would be a pity if gardeners became overly nervous about buying plants, and the best way to be confident in what you buy is to ask plenty of questions about sourcing. Although nurseries that sell organically certified plants are relatively rare, many nurseries, and in particular those

There are several options: ask about pesticides when you're buying and don't buy if nursery staff can't answer questions; choose an organic nursery, or a small independent where they raise the plants themselves and can tell you if they've been treated (and, if so, with what); swap plants with friends who grow organically, or grow your own from seed.

independents that grow their own plants, are happy to give customers information (while you're at it, check that they don't use peat or high levels of artificial fertilizers) – many are proud of their growing practices. Swaps with friends and neighbours who don't use chemicals are also a good source. And perhaps the easiest and cheapest way of all to get new plants is to grow from seed.

What is meant by a 'wildlife corridor'?

YOU'VE HEARD THE TERM used to refer to a whole range of spaces, from a hedge to an overgrown railway embankment; apparently even the local canal acts as a wildlife corridor. They're all broadly friendly to wildlife, but they're quite different in scale and nature, so what does 'wildlife corridor' actually mean?

Regardless of its scale, a wildlife corridor is a link between two or more larger areas of wildlife habitat, allowing creatures cover and safe passage to move between them undisturbed, thus avoiding isolation and inbreeding within local populations, and maximizing species diversity across a larger area. A wildlife corridor may be man-made or occur naturally.

As the human use of land has become more intensive, spaces previously serving as wildlife habitats have been cut up and, piecemeal, dedicated to farming or forestry, building or transport. All of these can break up the remaining areas of natural habitat, leaving 'islands' which, without wildlife corridors, could be isolated. They're sometimes also called green or habitat corridors, and even the word 'corridors' is a very wide definition that can be applied to a huge range of spaces, from a few shrubs growing along an urban pavement between city gardens, to a hedgerow that runs along the margins of a few cultivated fields, linking one woodland copse with another, all the way up to some much larger and longer 'corridors' on a grand scale, some of which can run for hundreds or even thousands of kilometres. Nor are they always land-based – rivers and canals can

Wildlife corridors in all their various forms create crucial links between areas of wildlife-friendly habitat that have been interrupted by human development.

be valuable water-based corridors, in particular through cities where links between wildlife-friendly areas may be thin.

Local corridors

At their most basic level, you can help to create new routes to serve as corridors in your immediate garden surroundings by leaving gaps or cutting doors in walls or fencing for frogs, toads and hedgehogs, and by letting edges of grass grow longer to afford small animals and insects safe passage between one space and another.

FROM IRON CURTAIN TO GREEN BELT

It's a far cry from a local hedgerow – as wildlife corridors go it's on a very large scale indeed. Reaching from Finland all the way south to Greece, the European Green Belt extends for nearly 12,500km (8,000 miles), following the line where the Iron Curtain used to be.

Ironically, one side effect of the Iron Curtain's watchtowers and no-go zones was the unwitting creation of a strip of land that escaped human traffic or cultivation. Even before the fall of the Berlin Wall, studies carried out by Friends of the Earth Germany in the no-man's-land it had created were showing a rich diversity of wildlife not present in the land either side of it, with species ranging from rare river mussels to otters, and black storks (pictured) to tiny midges. Sightings included more than 1,000 species from Germany's Red List, a national listing of endangered species.

Just one month after the opening of the border, a meeting of over 300 environmentalists from both East and West Germany passed a resolution to save this green belt from development and to extend it. Gradually the idea took shape and over the next 25 years, the European Green Belt came into being, comprising four sections – an uninterrupted strip of land dedicated to the interests of wildlife across 24 countries and across numerous habitats, from tundra and mountains to grasslands and bogs. Today, much of the belt encourages ecotourism and despite the fact that at its narrowest point it's only about 30m (100ft) wide, it's a stellar example of the way in which cooperation can create and enforce opportunities for wildlife.

Can wildlife gardens and kids mix?

IF YOU REMEMBER being entranced by frogs, baby birds and even worms when you were a small child, you want your children to feel the same enthusiasm for wildlife. What's the best way to ensure that the natural world can out-compete the small screen for their attention?

Beating nature deficit disorder

'Nature deficit disorder' is a term coined in 2006 by the US writer and journalist Richard Louv. His book, *Last Child in the Woods*, looked back to a past when children spent the majority of their free time outdoors and contrasted it with the lives of many of today's children, who he felt have little opportunity to explore the natural world and thus little awareness of it. He argued that the disconnect between children and nature was growing, and that strong links to the natural world are key to health as well

Wildlife is as absorbing as it ever was, but kids have to experience it first-hand to love it. And the easiest way is to 'get' them while they are still very young. Given the chance, and plenty of exposure, children love getting up close to wildlife, and the garden is the ideal place for them to learn.

as happiness in both children and adults. Reactions to his work led to the founding of an organization, the Children & Nature Network, which aims to reinforce the links between communities, children and the natural world, returning nature to its rightful place as a key part of childhood experience.

For everyday exposure to nature, nothing beats a garden. It's convenient and familiar; children can spend plenty of time exploring and observing in even a small garden, and its familiarity means that tiny changes – flowers and insects reappearing in spring, birds

▼ The tiny common shrew (*Sorex anaeus*), easily recognized by its pointed snout, is one of the small mammals that may take refuge in quiet corners of undergrowth.

visiting and, if you're lucky, nesting, and spiders' webs suddenly taking centre stage as autumn comes – are all highly visible. Make garden time with small children a daily routine, and travel round all potential habitats, from the compost bin to the woodpile and, if you have one, the pond, looking for any wildlife you can find. Back indoors, online resources can reinforce direct experience when you look things up together. Start early enough and you can spark a lifelong interest in the natural world, and a respect and value for the complex lifestyles of its myriad inhabitants.

SMALL-SCALE CHARISMA

Even the smallest child will have seen images of elephants, bears or tigers in their picture books or on a screen, yet comparatively few will see them in the wild. And on a smaller, more local scale, bees, butterflies, ladybirds, hedgehogs and frogs get plenty of exposure, too. But apart from occasional blockbusters like *The Very Hungry Caterpillar*, less immediately charismatic mini-beasts aren't often the stars of storybooks or cartoons, and thus don't often come within the average child's terms of reference unless they get the chance to observe them up close and personal in real life. Use the garden to broaden a child's scope: most kids are fascinated by tiny things, so invest in a couple of strong magnifying glasses and encourage children to look at small, exquisite insects such as lacewings, and at their monster-like larvae, or to sit very still and look at the

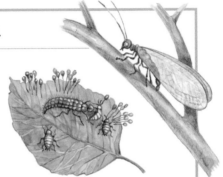

▲ The lacewing is one insect whose whole life cycle, from egg to larva to adult, can be observed in your garden.

'breathing' skin of a frog by the pond's edge; to admire the metallic wing covers of a beetle, or to watch pollinators in action around the flowers. Close-up, they'll find that even a tiger slug with its glistening stripes is (sort of) beautiful. Find out about invertebrate lifestyles and turn them into stories – a child who knows that a tadpole becomes a frog or that a caterpillar becomes a butterfly may be in the dark when it comes to how spiders or worms live and reproduce.

Do insects prefer 'native' plants?

YOU'VE PLANTED UP YOUR GARDEN with a wide range of flowering plants, with the idea of making it as friendly as possible to pollinators of all kinds. But should you take the geographical origin of your choice of plants into account, too?

Research by the Royal Horticultural Society (RHS) has found that the maximum number of pollinators in a UK garden was achieved with a broad mix of British 'natives' and other plants originating from the northern hemisphere, mixed in with a few 'exotics' with their origins in the southern hemisphere to extend the overall flowering season.

The importance of using mostly or in some cases exclusively 'native' species has been debated ever since the idea of gardening to benefit wildlife began, with many gardeners believing that invertebrates from a specific geographical area would prefer plants from the same geographical area. In Britain, the possible 'native' options are substantially fewer than in Europe – the typical British garden usually balances around 30 per cent native plant species against 70 per cent non-natives. With pollinators in decline, it's important to know how gardens can best provide the support they need. The Plants for Bugs study run by the RHS between 2010 and 2013 directed research at the native vs. non-native plants question with the aim of discovering which option was really best when it came both to pollinators and other invertebrates.

Three groups of flower beds were planted up with different sets of plants: British natives in one group, plants native to the northern hemisphere (excluding those native to Britain) in a second and 'exotics' (plants native to the southern hemisphere) in a third.

Bell heather (*Erica cinerea*) is a native plant, rich in nectar and with a long flowering season – excellent value for pollinators.

Pollinators and others

The findings looked first at which group of plants attracted the highest number of flower-visiting insects (or pollinators) and second at the results for those invertebrates who lived on the plants but aren't pollinators. The findings in relation to the pollinating insects concluded that native British plants only had about a 10 per cent advance on plants from the northern hemisphere when it came to their popularity with pollinators; exotics fell a little further behind, but were valued for their tendency to flower later into the season than the other two groups.

What about the non-pollinators?

When it came to non-pollinating invertebrates that lived on the plants such as caterpillars, aphids and spiders, native plant species supported slightly more invertebrates – a bit less than 10 per cent – than northern hemisphere plants, and about 20 per cent more than plants from the southern hemisphere. Density of planting was a key factor: the more thickly planted a plot, the more invertebrates it will support, regardless of where the plants originate.

BEST PRACTICE TO BENEFIT POLLINATORS

• Aim for a long flowering season: the more plants are in flower across the longest period of time, the better it is for pollinating insects. Attempt to have some plants in flower every month of the year.

• Go for density: the more flowers there are, the more pollinators they'll attract.

• Grow a variety: it's unnecessary to limit yourself to growing native plants only. Aim for a good selection of native plants, backed up with other plants from the northern hemisphere, and include some late-flowering species from the southern hemisphere (such as *Verbena bonariensis*, pictured) to give you – and the pollinators – a longer flowering season.

• And finally, believe the evidence of your eyes: if you see a plant or plants that seems to be particularly popular with pollinators, plant more of it.

Can a container-only garden help wildlife?

YOU HAVE A SMALL, HARD-SURFACE yard or balcony – is it worth trying to turn it into a wildlife oasis when you're confined to container-only gardening?

When it comes to what to choose for your containers, look to plants that will cover a long flowering season – choose carefully and you can have a succession of containers in flower from the end of winter to late the following autumn.

Grow herbs

Add a few pots of herbs. They're easy to grow, they smell good, they're useful in the kitchen and, if left to flower, most are excellent for pollinating insects as well. Mints, thymes, lavender, rosemary (pictured), oregano and borage are just a few possibilities.

Dahlias

The many-layered varieties of show dahlias don't have very much to offer pollinators, but it's a different story with the simple single-flowered (as above) or semi-double-flowered varieties, with their open centres and easily accessible pollen and nectar, which can more than pay their way. Dahlias are greedy with water, but with regular deadheading they flower prolifically and are popular with bees. Unless your yard or balcony is very sheltered, the tubers should be stored indoors or in a frost-free shed in winter.

Planted up right, container gardens can be valuable wildlife resources wherever they are. Nectar- and pollen-rich plants will benefit visiting pollinators who can fly into an environment without needing cover to get there. Provide a container water feature, or, even smaller, a bee drinker (see pp109) and you'll broaden the wildlife appeal even more.

FIVE TOP CONTAINER PLANTS FOR POLLINATORS

Plants that are beautiful for you and beneficial for a range of pollinators, including bees, hoverflies and butterflies.

Sarcococca ruscifolia var. chinensis **'Dragon Gate'** A glossy evergreen shrub which will grow up to 1m (3ft) tall in a large container and which offers small, white scented flowers at the end of winter, which are appreciated by early-emerging bees when not much else is in flower.

Verbena rigida Hardy garden verbena has scented purple flowers on tall branched stems. In northern climates it's usually grown as an annual, with a flowering season that will stretch from June to November, although if your yard is very sheltered, it may overwinter successfully. It can reach 1m (3ft) in height and is especially popular with butterflies.

Erysimum **'Bowles Mauve'** An evergreen purplish-mauve wallflower which will stay in bloom for an extraordinarily long season in a sheltered spot and will last for several years in a container. Height is 0.5–1m (1½–3ft), and it appeals to a wide range of pollinators.

Cosmos bipinnatus **'Apollo Carmine'** A half-hardy annual cosmos that can easily be grown from seed and is short enough to work well in a container without flopping – it reaches about 65cm (2ft). The flowers are a deep magenta with a bright yellow centre and, with regular deadheading, will keep going from June until October.

Rudbeckia hirta **'Toto'** This short biennial rudbeckia has vivid yellow daisy-like flowers with chocolate-brown centres. With a maximum height of 50cm (1½ft), it's short enough to grow easily in a container, and it flowers relatively late, extending the season into autumn with flowers for you and pollen and nectar for insects.

Garden cosmos,
Cosmos bipinnatus

Is recycling part of wildlife gardening?

BY ITS VERY NATURE, gardening is a constant recycling process: dead plant matter goes to compost to feed the next generation of plants, while flowers give way to fruit, which in turn supplies seed to grow the next generation. But if, to you, 'recycling' in the garden has only ever meant planters made from car tyres (and of course there's nothing wrong with that if you like them), are there other recycling ideas that won't make your garden look like a dump?

Almost every gardener already repurposes and recycles – whether starting off sweet peas or runner beans in toilet rolls or using plastic bottles with the bases cut off as cloches around tender seedlings! Large quantities of garden waste can be recycled on site: spare wood can make a log pile, swept leaves will make leaf mould and all kinds of waste can go to compost.

Make your own compost bin

If you like a project, one genuinely useful (and easy) possibility is a compost bin made using old wooden pallets. You can usually get these for free from construction sites or supermarkets (do ask and check they're not wanted – don't just remove pallets propped against skips, for example). Avoid any that are stamped with the letters 'MB': these are old pallets that have been treated with methyl bromide, and they aren't suitable for garden use.

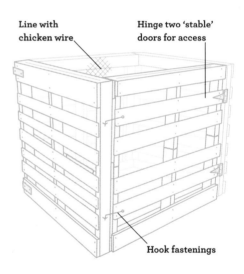

Line with chicken wire

Hinge two 'stable' doors for access

Hook fastenings

You need four pallets, ideally the same size, a drill, a saw, corner brackets, two hinges, two hook-and-eye fixings and screws. Start by fixing three of the pallets together in a U-shape using the brackets, then saw the fourth in half widthways. This will make the stable-door front to the bin, which is divided into two halves to make it easier to turn your compost and get it out of the container when it's ready. Attach the top and bottom halves of the door to the side of the container with the hinges and fix the hooks to the door and the eyes to the side of the bin where the door meets it.

Pallets have quite wide gaps in their sides, which is fine for coarse gardening trimmings. If you'll be adding a lot of smaller material you can avoid pieces falling out by wrapping the inside or outside of the new compost bin in chicken wire, tacking it down at the corners.

A Looking to reuse and recycle rather than always buy new is as much a part of wildlife gardening as any other. Plenty of recycling consists of basic shortcuts, so always check any make-do-and-mend solutions before going shopping. Nature has supplied the ultimate recycling model in the shape of the millions of decomposers who live in your garden soil.

NATURAL RECYCLERS: DECOMPOSERS

You may never have given much thought to why we're not up to our eyes with dead material in the garden. You sweep up leaves and put a certain proportion of plant clippings and other material into the compost, but all your garden detritus, wherever you put it, will disappear eventually. Your take on it is that it 'rots down': what's actually happening is that it's being recycled by decomposers. Decomposers may be fungi, bacteria, actinomycetes (which, confusingly, look like fungi but are actually bacteria) or detritivores, and most of them live in the soil. You have to take the smaller decomposers on trust, as the vast majority are far too small to see, but they're the ultimate recyclers, taking dead or rotting organisms and transforming them into simpler substances. The populations of these smaller lifeforms are vast: 1m by 1m (1$\frac{1}{2}$ft by 1$\frac{1}{2}$ft) of soil may contain 10 trillion bacteria and actinomycetes, 5,000,000 nematodes and a mere 60,000 springtails, the tiny jumpers that you'll most often spot in your compost heap.

▼ Inkcap mushrooms (*Parasola auricoma*): some of the more visible of the trillions of species who work at decomposing dead plant material.

Need I worry about kids' safety in the garden?

YOU'RE KEEN FOR YOUR CHILDREN to get to know the natural world close up, and you want a wildlife garden with all the kinds of habitat you can fit in. How big a worry is safety – if you're vigilant when everyone is out in the garden, do you need to take any other precautions?

As the natural world has become a smaller part of everyday life for most people, its dangers have tended to become exaggerated. But a garden isn't really any more hazardous for children than a house: the former may have poisonous or spiky plants and insects that could sting, but the latter has plug sockets or other potential hazards that we are so used to looking out for that they hardly register. Take the same approach to the garden as you would to the house: be vigilant but let your children explore without panic.

Very small children need to be under your eye all the time. When

Very small children shouldn't be left unattended in the garden any more than you would leave them alone in the house. Water is the biggest danger: with smaller kids, it may be sensible to limit yourself to small water features or a bog garden, graduating to a pond when they're a little older.

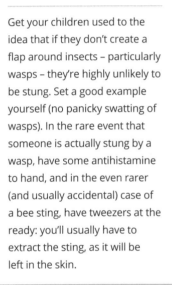

INSECT STINGS

Get your children used to the idea that if they don't create a flap around insects – particularly wasps – they're highly unlikely to be stung. Set a good example yourself (no panicky swatting of wasps). In the rare event that someone is actually stung by a wasp, have some antihistamine to hand, and in the even rarer (and usually accidental) case of a bee sting, have tweezers at the ready: you'll usually have to extract the sting, as it will be left in the skin.

they're a bit older, drill them in the basics (they shouldn't put anything in their mouth, they shouldn't go near water). By the time they're aged around six they are usually old enough to do some exploring on their own – and if you were worried about water before, this is probably also the age when you can safely graduate to a pond.

Are lawns good for wildlife, or is a border better?

WHICH IS THE 'BEST' HABITAT for a wildlife gardener to encourage? Should you go for grass (including some that's been left to grow long), or a border full of pollinator-pleasing plants?

There isn't really a 'best' in this context: a variety of habitats is good, because habitats outside the garden are generally tending to become more uniform. The strength gardens have is their capacity to offer lots of different habitats within a relatively small area.

Is messy more appealing than tidy?

Will a manicured lawn with a number 2 cut appeal to as many species as some grass left to grow long and tussocky? No, nor will an immaculate border where every plant is surrounded by a neat circle of bare earth suit most invertebrate species as well as a densely planted one which offers lots of foliage cover as well as flowers. But it's a widely disseminated myth that a garden needs to be messy to appeal to wildlife – it needs to be planted with the widest possible range of plants and shrubs and it's best left with some undisturbed corners.

IF I PLANT IT, WILL THEY COME?

You've created a great habitat with the right plants, so can you now expect all the species associated with that habitat to appear? Yes and no. If you plant the right things, wildlife will often start using your space. But you can't expect all of it. Unlike a zoo, wildlife has to come to you, it isn't collected and delivered there, and the rarest creatures are rare for a reason. Maybe they like a seldom-occurring and fast-vanishing sort of habitat, maybe they aren't able to fly long distances to seek it out, or maybe you're in the wrong part of the country and thus don't have the right weather – it's too cold or too wet – for that species to live there. Creating different habitats in a garden is important for biodiversity, but that doesn't mean that every possible species will come.

Should I keep a wildlife record?

YOU'RE A KEEN WILDLIFE GARDENER but your style is fairly ad hoc; would an annual record – maybe a combination of wildlife sightings and planting notes – be helpful for planning? What's the best way to set about it?

Find your own style

Gardening records are very personal, and you'll find which way works for you when you start: you may like a handwritten notebook, bursting with extra clippings and plant and wildlife information gleaned from all kinds of sources; you may prefer neat files printed out on spreadsheets with meticulous dating and observation notes, or you may go for something in between.

Whatever kind of record style you pick, add pictures – keep your phone nearby when you're spending time in the garden so that you can take a snap when you spot a new or unusual species. You'll find the record most useful if there aren't long gaps: aim to update whenever you're in the garden for more than a minute or two (enthusiasts may end up updating several times daily, especially in spring, when it can seem as though there are dozens of small happenings going on all the time). Stick to a few standard headings for each entry, alongside the date, to make it easy to find specific items when you're looking back.

Wildlife watch over time

Maintaining wildlife records for the same space over several years offers lots of interest when you look back: you see the differences made to the range of species you spot by unusually wet or hot years, or the addition of new features (perhaps a pond, or a woodpile), the dates on which visiting birds began nesting, or caterpillar sightings went up when you researched and grew some potential food plants. Tracking the changes in the seasons across a number of years may also give you a sense of how climate change is affecting the

◄ Keep your phone at hand so that you can take quick snaps of different species as you spot them: they won't hang around while you go to fetch it.

weather. Full records give you an intimate view into how your garden has changed (and hopefully become more and more appealing to a diverse range of species) across a period of time. Make sure that you take pictures of the whole garden from various viewpoints, at least annually or perhaps seasonally, so you get an overview.

Spotting for kids

Wildlife notebooks are often popular with children – they'll enjoy being able to keep their own record, and if they seem interested you can set them up with a book or folder at the same time as you start yours. Smaller children can draw what they see. If you need a garden activity, offer them a home-made game of wildlife bingo. It's easy to make: print out snaps of 6 or 9 wildlife species, from woodlice to ants, with one or two more challenging ones

A wildlife notebook, whether kept on paper or online, is the best way to remind you what you've accomplished in your garden. It's invaluable for keeping an accurate record, year-on-year, of wildlife sightings, complete with photos where possible. Plant- and habitat-wise, it's also useful for remembering what you planted and which species liked what.

(check with your own records that there's a reasonable chance of spotting them so that they're not too difficult). Stick them down on plain postcards, give each player some coloured sticky 'spotter's dots' and offer a small prize to whoever spots all the species first.

WHAT TO RECORD?

Start with a date, then have headings covering mammals, birds, reptiles, amphibians and invertebrates.

Note down the time of day or night you saw them, what they were doing, and identifying features, particularly with some of the smaller and harder-to-identify species of invertebrates. Include labelled pictures if you can.

Apart from the sighting information, have a page opposite for general notes – this might cover signs of nest building by birds and the materials they were selecting, the species name of a particular plant that appears to be attracting a very high share of different pollinators, a spotting of the first spider's web in the autumn garden, and so on.

Is it worth setting up a trailcam or a nest box camera?

IF YOU'RE A DEVOTEE OF NATURE PROGRAMMES, it's tempting to set up a live show streamed from your own garden. There's a wide choice of potential stars, from the foxes who visit nightly to the blue tits who set up home annually in your bird box. How complicated are trailcams or nest box cameras to set up, and how much can you expect to see of the private lives of your wildlife?

▲ Word-of-mouth is the best recommendation if you want a trailcam: ask around friends who use them, and perhaps borrow before you buy.

Trailcams

A trail-camera is really easy to set up: most are ready to use straight away, out of the box. It's battery-operated, triggered by motion sensors and is easy to move around the garden. You can put out food to attract your nocturnal wildlife to various different sites in your garden and see which position gets you the best results. The images are recorded onto a memory card and can then be downloaded and viewed on a computer or TV – most trailcams record both stills and video footage and can be set to record different periods of time. Although trailcams are available at a range of prices, there's very little variation in the way they work. The more expensive versions will give you higher-quality images. If you're buying, get one that is 'waterproof' rather than 'splashproof' to make sure it won't suffer if there's heavy rain overnight (you can also build it a small 'shelter' of propped bricks or tiles if it doesn't look terribly durable).

Nest box cameras

These are more complicated to set up than trailcams. There are wired and wireless versions of the box-with-camera-ready-installed available, although reports suggest that the former tend to work better. The wired kind needs to be connected to your computer or a TV by cables which can be passed through an air vent; they can be slightly fiddly to install if you're not a DIY maven. Once up and working, if your box gets tenants, a nest box camera will give you a uniquely personal view of the whole process, from nest building to incubating the clutch and all the stages of the chicks growing and fledging – and you'll probably find that you become deeply invested in the success of the brood. The downside is that you're not guaranteed to attract birds to the nesting box – remember that the nature programmes on TV ensure that they get the great footage you see by having dozens of different cameras at different sites and in various combinations, whereas your single domestic setup may not succeed every season. To give it the best chance, site the box in your garden at a spot where birds have nested in previous years and set it up well in advance of nesting season, bearing in mind that early birds, blue tits for

A Neither trailcams nor nest box cameras need be expensive, although both are available in different 'grades' and, as you'd expect, to an extent you get what you pay for. If you're new to nest box cameras it's usually simpler to buy the box and camera as a single unit. Both offer intriguing glimpses of garden wildlife behaving as it does when you're not there.

example, may already be scoping out likely nesting sites by the beginning of February.

PEREGRINE VS. PARAKEET

We've become used to nest box cameras offering us footage of many species of birds, from robins and tits to falcons and owls, that can be watched online. Along the way, they have contributed greatly to our knowledge of the habits of different species. For example, the ring-necked parakeet (*Psittacula krameri*), the small, green parrot with the vivid red beak that has been one of the most successful recent avian incomers in European cities – to the extent that it's considered a pest in many places – has also apparently become a popular item in the diet of the peregrine falcon. (A recent study of London birds revealed that hobbies and tawny owls are also partial to a meal of parakeet.) While a few falcons have been spotted in the act of taking them, the most revealing giveaway was the rather macabre sight, captured on a nestcam set up next to a peregrine nest, of a line-up of small, bright red beaks at the nest's edge: all that was left of the original owners after the falcons had dined.

Should I get rid of decking?

DECKING IN THE GARDEN enjoyed a huge boom in the 1990s and early 2000s; more recently, though, it's been called into question because of the valuable habitat it takes from wildlife in the garden. Does it have any redeeming features or is it best to get rid of it?

While the crawl space under decking may sometimes be taken over by foxes (or, less appealingly, rats) and occasionally may offer a nest for a hedgehog, decking itself has little to recommend it wildlife-wise. The best solution is to take it out and plant up the ground space you're left with.

If removing the decking isn't an option, next best is to plant up plenty of containers with pollinator-friendly plants. But if you can remove it, do: even if you opt to pave or brick over the earth underneath, these surfaces don't smother growing opportunities in the same way as decking, because they're laid directly over the soil (or over a layer of sand on the soil), offering potential growing gaps at the edges and between

WHAT ABOUT ARTIFICIAL GRASS?

As the trend for decking seems to be drawing gradually to a close, the fashion for artificial turf is on the rise. Although one reason often cited for installing it is that it survives the heavy footfall of children better than the real thing, there are tough lawn grasses available which can cope with heavy traffic at no cost to wildlife. Not only does it not offer any wildlife benefits, but it is made of polymers, its production is environmentally unfriendly and, when worn out, it creates waste that isn't biodegradable.

bricks and stones. Even better, dig and plant up the freed space once the decking is gone.

Can I attract pollinators in a shady garden?

LIGHT SHADE, especially mixed with sunny areas, isn't too much of a problem when it comes to encouraging wildlife into the garden. But are there any pollinators that actually prefer it to full sun?

While pollinators usually prefer to forage in sunshine, the speckled wood butterfly (*Pararge aegeria*), a prettily marked butterfly with rows of black and gold 'eyes' along the edges of its hind-wings, is one that flies happily in shade, as does the ringlet (*Aphantopus hyperantus*, pictured), a velvety brown butterfly with fine white edgings to its wings and five gold-rimmed 'rings' on the underside of its hind wings. Other butterflies that may fly in shade as well as sun include the comma (*Polygonia c-album*) – easily recognized by its orange and brown colouring and deeply scalloped wings – and the vivid green brimstone (*Gonepteryx rhamni*).

In terms of planting, species that grow at a woodland's edge and can cope with dappled shade are the best choices. While shade isn't popular with many pollinators, a select range of butterflies favour it, and some other invertebrates, including ground beetles, will seek it out.

GOOD POLLINATOR PLANTS FOR DAPPLED SHADE

Pulmonaria 'Blue Ensign' All lungworts grow well in semi-shade, and the vivid purple-blue flowers of this variety have a strong attraction for pollinators.

Digitalis purpurea f. *albiflora* The classic white foxglove which can look almost luminous in dappled shade.

Sweet cicely (*Myrrhis odorata*) Ferny leaves and umbellifers of small white flowers.

Campanula persicifolia A perennial that forms rosettes from which narrow, wiry stalks emerge, carrying bell-shaped, gentian-blue flowers from late spring into summer.

We hear a lot about species declines, but is there any good news for wildlife?

MANY SCIENTISTS SUGGEST that Earth is already in the throes of a 'mass extinction event' – something so cataclysmic that it will have ecological, economic and social consequences that are beyond anything that is predictable or even imaginable to us today. But at the same time, it's reported that some species are thriving, so is it all bad news for wildlife?

What is a mass extinction event?

Academics agree that Earth has already seen five mass extinction events: the disagreement comes as to whether or not we are beginning on, or even midway through, a sixth. The first on record, in the late Devonian period, an almost unimaginably remote 360 million years ago, is believed to have rendered 70 per cent of the species alive on Earth extinct. The fifth and most recent, the Cretaceous-Tertiary extinction, a mere 65 million years ago, was the one that saw the end of the age of the dinosaurs, allowing mammals, and eventually humans, to evolve. As you'd deduce from its name, a mass extinction event sees the extinction of at least 70 per cent and often more of the species alive at the time over a very brief period and – as you'd expect – such an event invariably has a huge effect on those species remaining. Humans have changed the world very much, very fast: our activities are responsible for habitat loss, pollution on a massive scale and global warming, and our ascendance hasn't been good news for most other species. One shocking study, which was produced for the World Wildlife Fund and published in 2018, demonstrated that around 50 per cent of the global animal population was lost between 1970 and 2014.

Green matters aren't ever black and white, and the vastly differing scales of the global, national and local pictures can make for confusing and sometimes conflicting news reports. On the local scale, there are still wildlife successes to report, but the larger picture remains undeniably worrying.

There's an interesting counter-argument, though. One that proposes that the disruptive effects of human activity can also encourage biodiversity, as species faced with new situations or brought together from different parts of the world are creating hybrids. This argument says that we depend too much on the ecological and environmental status quo, and that it's unrealistic to expect that things won't change.

Thinking positive

Whichever argument you prefer, and most would find the second one at least offers some optimism, it's important to remember that individual efforts still count. We can concentrate in promoting biodiversity in whatever way and at whatever scale we can, even if that's simply promoting the interests of as broad a range of species as possible in your back garden.

MAKING A DIFFERENCE

If you were searching for a bit of good news, a study drawn up by the British Ornithology Trust looks at the population increases of specific bird species across the last 50 years. Many of the populations of the 29 species listed are expected to go up rather than down over the next few years, including birds that traditionally live in hedgerows or in the margins of woodland, for example the nuthatch, the wren, the long-tailed and great tits, the blackcap and the robin, to name just a few. And the reason that these birds appear to be enjoying a modest boom may be that they have been able to take full advantage of the increased feeding opportunities in gardens: an encouraging thought for anyone who has ever wondered if their efforts at finding and feeding appropriate food to the visitors to their bird table are actually worth it.

▼ Wrens (*Troglodytes troglodytes*), originally most often found in woodland and hedgerows, have benefited from the increase in garden habitats.

Further reading

An Ear to the Ground: Garden Science for Ordinary Mortals
Ken Thompson
Transworld Publishers, 2003

Bob's Basics: Composting
Bob Flowerdew
Kyle Books, 2010

Butterfly Gardening
Jenny Steel
Brambleby Books, 2016

Charles Dowding's Vegetable Garden Diary: No Dig, Healthy Soil, Fewer Weeds (2nd edition)
Charles Dowding
No Dig Garden, 2017

Companion to Wildlife Gardening
Chris Baines
Frances Lincoln, 2016

Dream Plants for the Natural Garden
Piet Oudolf and Henk Gerritsen
Frances Lincoln, 2013

RHS Encyclopedia of Gardening
Christopher Brickell
Dorling Kindersley, 2012

Gardening for Wildlife
Adrian Thomas
Bloomsbury Publishing, 2017

Good Soil: Manure, Compost and Nourishment for Your Garden
Tina Råman
Frances Lincoln, 2017

RHS How Do Worms Work?
Guy Barter
Mitchell Beazley, 2016

How to Create an Eco Garden: The Practical Guide to Greener, Planet-Friendly Gardening
John Walker
Aquamarine, 2011

Insects of Britain and Northern Europe
Michael Chinery
Collins Field Guides, 1993

Life in the Soil: A Guide for Naturalists and Gardeners
James B. Nardi
University of Chicago Press, 2007

Making Wildlife Ponds
Jenny Steel
Brambleby Books, 2016

A Natural History of the Hedgerow
John Wright
Profile Books, 2016

No Nettles Required
Ken Thompson
Eden Project Books, 2006

RHS Pests & Diseases: The Definitive Guide to Prevention and Treatment (2nd edition)
Pippa Greenwood and Andrew Halstead
Dorling Kindersley, 2018

Planting: A New Perspective
Piet Oudolf and Noel Kingsbury
Timber Press, 2013

The Sceptical Gardener
Ken Thompson
Icon Books, 2016

The Secret Life of Flies
Erica McAlister
The Natural History Museum, 2017

Still Water: The Deep Life of the Pond
John Lewis-Stempel
Doubleday, 2019

Where Do Camels Belong?
Ken Thompson
Profile Books, 2014

The Wildlife Gardener
Kate Bradbury
Pen and Sword Books, 2017

Wildlife Gardening for Everyone and Everything
Kate Bradbury
Bloomsbury Publishing, 2019

About the authors

Helen Bostock is the Senior Horticultural Advisor at the RHS and has more than a decade's experience working in the Advisory Service.

Sophie Collins has authored more than 20 books and this one offered a great chance to combine her twin interests in wildlife and gardening in a single title.

Isabella Tree is an award-winning author, travel writer, and owner of the Knepp Wildland Project. She is the author of several books, including *Wilding, The Return of Nature to a British Farm* (Picador, 2019).

Index

Credits